INTERACTIVE SYSTEM

ISBN: 978-0-244-74676-6

Andreas Sofroniou, 2019 © Copyright

Andreas Sofroniou, 2019 © Copyright

INTERACTIVE SYSTEMS

ISBN: 978-0-244-74676-6

Contents

Page

Andreas Sofroniou

Interactions of major systems

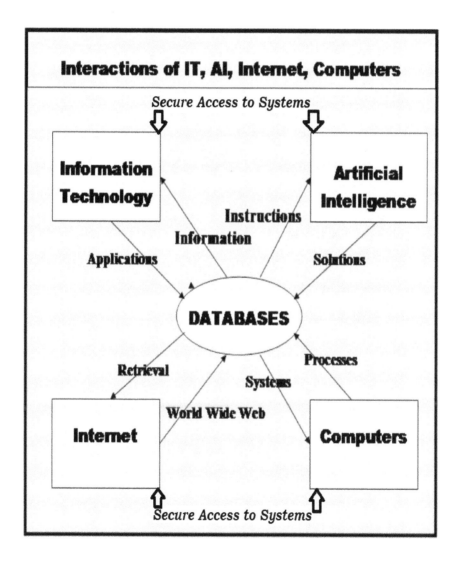

Systems Interaction

Response to Instructions

An interactive system is a computer system which responds to instructions from the user as they are given. The system responds fast enough to allow transactions to be completed almost continuously.

The success or failure of each transaction is immediately obvious from the way in which the computer responds. The instructions are input via a device such as a mouse or keyboard.

While the precise structure of the future interactive systems is not yet clear, many directions of growth seem apparent. One is the increased availability of wireless access. Wireless services enable applications not previously possible in any economical fashion.

Global positioning systems (GPS) combined with wireless Internet access would help mobile users to locate alternate routes, generate precise accident reports, initiate recovery services, and improve traffic management and congestion control.

In addition to wireless laptop computers and personal digital assistants (PDAs), wearable devices with voice input and special display glasses are available with further facilities under development.

6

Communications and exchange of information

Communications deal with the mutual exchange of information between technological devices and individuals; a process central to human experience and social organization.

The study of communication involves many disciplines, including technology, linguistics, psychology, sociology, and anthropology. All forms of communication, from interpersonal to mass media communications, involve an initiator, who formulates a message and sends it as a signal, by means of a particular channel, to a receiver, who decodes and interprets the meaning.

In interpersonal communication involving face-to-face conversation, communication is direct, using the code of language, and reinforced by non-verbal communication such as body movement, eye contact, gesture, and facial expression. Response is also direct. Interpersonal communication can also take place at a distance.

Other forms of communications use writing and printing as the means of conveying messages.

The invention of the printing press was the first step in the development of mass communication (publishing). Books, newspapers, and periodicals are able to convey messages to a wide audience; an even wider audience is reached by radio and television, film, and the recording industries.

The mass media and the arts impose their own codes and characteristics on to their messages, which can range from relatively straightforward ideological tracts to complex texts carrying multiple layers of possible meaning.

7

Communications revolution

The communications revolution is an unprecedented advance in the speed of message transmission.

In 1794 the French army started to use semaphore to pass messages, and a hot-air balloon to observe the enemy. In 1837 Charles Wheatstone in Britain and Samuel Morse in the USA developed an electric telegraph, the latter sending electric signals by means of a 'Morse-code'. Telegraph lines were erected between Washington and Baltimore in 1844, then across Europe, and in 1866 across the Atlantic.

One of the effects of the telegraph was that it linked international banking; another was that newspapers could print up-to-date international news; thirdly, governments could exert much closer control, for example in war or in their distant colonies.

With the telephone (1876) direct speech communication replaced the telegram, while radio (1899) removed the need for communicants to be linked by electric cables. Television (1926) enabled visual images to be transmitted, while satellites (from the 1970s) enabled the whole world to watch events of supranational interest, with English becoming increasingly the language of the world.

In the 1980s information technology emerged as a computer-based means of storing and transmitting information using networks of computers linked together, especially for academic or business use. The networks were subsequently connected into a global system using fibre-optic cables and existing telephone channels.

During the 1990s, the use of this system, known as the Internet, expanded dramatically with an increase in the ownership of personal computers. The Internet came to be used for transmitting electronic mail, accessing and exchanging information, electronic on-line publishing, and, to some extent, entertainment.

Input device

The input device in computing is a peripheral which allows information from an external source to be fed into a computer system.

The standard input device for most modern computer systems is a keyboard, similar to a typewriter's but with additional keys which provide a larger range of characters and control functions. Many computers are also equipped with a mouse.

Before the advent of interactive systems, computers used punched card or paper-tape readers as their standard input devices.

Many different input devices are available for more specialist applications. Scanners, digitizers, or even video cameras are used for graphics systems. Point-of-sale terminals may have bar-code readers.

Optical character recognition systems are used in banking, to read codes printed on cheques, or in desk-top publishing systems to convert printed documents into ASCII codes so that they can be stored and processed digitally.

Peripherals

A peripheral in computing is a device that is connected to a computer system but is not part of the central processing unit or associated memory. Common peripherals include output devices such as printers and plotter units, disk drives, input devices such as keyboards attached to visual display units, and modems.

9

Peripherals usually require hardware and software interfaces to function under control of the computer's operating system. The interface circuits ensure that information is transferred from the central processing unit in the correct way, and that input data is correctly received.

Memory

Memory (in computing) is that part of a computer system that is used to store data temporarily or permanently. There are many types of computer memory, each with a specific application. Most types of computer memory are made from semiconductors.

For very high-speed operations associated with the central processing unit (CPU), real (primary) memory is used. This includes read-only memory (ROM) and random access memory (RAM).

Information is stored permanently in a ROM and cannot normally be altered once programmed, but various types of erasable programmable ROM (EPROM) are now quite common. Computers use ROM-based information for some essential tasks such as bootstrapping.

The operating system and some small programs may also be stored in ROM. RAMs are used for short-term storage of information and programs, including instructions, data, and partial results, and are intimately associated with the high-speed operation of the CPU. Virtual (secondary) memory is not directly addressable by the CPU, but is used to store much larger amounts of data, although this is only accessible at relatively low speeds compared with the operation of the computer. It usually resides on disk units such as hard and floppy disks.

Large programs can be run on computers using a relatively small amount of real memory, by continually exchanging information between real memory and a hard disk (containing the virtual memory) so that only those parts of the program currently in use take up space in real memory.

Cache memory is a small but very fast memory interposed between a computer and its main memory. The computer first checks whether data is in the cache before going to the (relatively slow) main memory.

In operation, the CPU controls the read and write operations of memory and the transfer of data between real and virtual memories.

A new erasable computer memory chip made partly from a ceramic, and known as a ferroelectric random-access memory (FRAM) is under development. It retains data when its power source is switched off, and could eventually replace ROM and RAM.

Visual display unit

A menu is a list of program or function options which is presented to the user by a computer on a visual display unit. The user selects the desired option by keyboard or mouse. Menu-based software is used extensively in interactive systems because of its convenience and ease of use.

11

Technological revolutions

Technological advances

Technological revolutions include a series of technological advances made in the latter half of the 20th century in the manufacturing industries, agriculture, medicine, communications (communications revolution), energy supply, and warfare.

The changes to national economies caused by the Industrial Revolution and automation were greatly enhanced by the development of high-technology industry since World War II. The productivity, prosperity, and economic growth of nations came to reflect the wealth or otherwise of their electronic, aerospace, chemical, and biotechnological industries. Their national security depended on advanced military technology for weapons and intelligence.

Health care increasingly came to depend on sophisticated instruments and treatment as well as on advanced pharmaceuticals. Information was spread around the world through a network of complex telecommunications.

Employment in the service and manufacturing sector came to depend on computers and automation. Even the quality of leisure time became, in the technologically advanced nations, based on consumer electronics and on the technological feats of the entertainment industry.

Investment in high-technology industry enabled first Japan, the USA, and Europe, and thereafter countries of the Pacific Rim of East Asia (e.g. South Korea, Taiwan), to achieve unprecedented prosperity. By contrast, the economies of the former communist nations, which had invested primarily in obsolescent heavy manufacturing plant and arms manufacture, became non-viable.

12

Today, the world market for the electronics industry alone is worth billions, and is expected to be trillions in the next few years. With markets now increasingly competitive, future development in technology is seen in terms of the formation of global consortia, alliances, and collaborations which co-operate and compete at the same time.

Communications satellite

The communications satellite is an artificial satellite for world-wide telephone, television, and data communication; using microwaves (electromagnetic radiation). Microwaves can carry vast amounts of information because of their large bandwidth and suitability for multiplexing.

They are, however, easily absorbed by solid objects, so transmitter and receiver need to be in line of sight. Satellites provide a method of achieving line-of-sight communication over long distances: world-wide coverage can be achieved using as few as three satellites.

The USA's *Echo 1* (1960) was the first satellite designed for radio communication experiments. Because *Echo 1* was merely a reflector, its signals were very weak. In 1962 the Bell Telephone Company launched *Telstar*, an active satellite carrying its own solar power source for signal amplification, which enabled the first live television broadcast from the USA to Europe to be made. Because the ground station's antennae could only 'see' the satellite for about 20 minutes on each orbit, that was the length of the broadcast.

By 1963 rockets sufficiently powerful to place a satellite in geostationary orbit were available. *Syncom 1*, a US satellite for telephone and telex use, was the first geostationary satellite. The first commercial geostationary satellite was *Early Bird* or *Intelsat 1*, launched in 1965 by the International Telecommunications Satellite Organization.

13

Intelsat soon had three satellites over the Atlantic, Pacific, and Indian Oceans for world-wide coverage, and today numerous communications satellites orbit the Earth. Modern communications satellites can handle tens of thousands of telephone calls, plus radio and television broadcasts.

Navigation satellite

The navigation satellite is a radio aid to navigation using artificial satellites orbiting the Earth.

Such satellites are used by ships, aircraft, missiles, or land vehicles (especially military vehicles) to find their position, height, and speed. The first practical system in operation was developed by the US Navy and known as Transit. It became available for commercial use in 1967.

A more sophisticated US system, the Navstar Global Positioning System (GPS), will be fully operational in the mid-1990s. The GPS satellites carry atomic clocks and daily transmit their position and time to ground stations.

The Soviet Union had its own system, and there are also commercial systems that operate using existing communications satellites. The GPS has satellites in uniformly spaced geostationary orbits above the Earth.

Commercial navigational receivers that use signals from GPS are now being used to make small accurate navigational devices. Navigation systems for boats, aircraft, and cars are widely available.

14

Information Technology (IT)

Application of systems

Information technology is the umbrella term used to describe the practical applications of computer systems. The term has become prevalent with the increasing use of computers such as word processors for office systems, but it also embraces the more traditional areas of data processing and information retrieval.

Key factors in the recent rapid spread of microelectronics and information technology (often known simply as 'new technology') have been the drastic reduction in electronic hardware costs during the 1970s and 1980s; the so-called 'convergence' of computing and telecommunications (historically denoted by the term telematics); and the emergence of various formal standards and informal agreements within the IT industry.

The mass production of microprocessors and other electronic components at low unit cost has made it possible to incorporate digital electronics into a wide range of products for commerce, industry, and the home.

New technology has made an enormous impact on the design and performance of consumer goods, for example, cameras, video and hi-fi equipment, and personal computers.

In offices and business, new technology was introduced for text processing, using dedicated (special-purpose) word processors. Now, however, it is usual to find general-purpose small computers and workstations being exploited for a much wider range of office applications using special-purpose application software such as financial planning packages, management support software, information storage and retrieval applications, desk-top publishing, and so on.

Expert systems using artificial intelligence techniques to aid decision-making can also be run on suitable personal computers.

Networks

The combination of computing with private and public telecommunication networks has been particularly significant in retailing and banking. Bar codes on products can be read automatically at check-outs, and the information used both to print a customer's receipt and to reorder necessary stocks.

Electronic funds transfer using an 'intelligent' cash register or point-of-sale terminal can then complete the cycle of electronic information flow by automatically debiting the customer's bank or credit-card account by the appropriate amount.

Sales records held by the store's central computer can be used to develop overall retailing strategies; records of the purchasing patterns of particular customers can be exploited for direct marketing of goods or services.

Manufacturing and processing

The IT revolution has been just as great in the manufacturing and processing industries. An early application was the numerical control of machine-tools, in which digital electronics were used to control lathes and other equipment. Now it has become common for a wide range of industrial equipment (sensors, control systems, robots, and so on) to incorporate microelectronics and to be interconnected (networked) so that information can be gathered, communicated, and processed in order to optimize the activity.

Artificial intelligence, in which computer programs mimic certain aspects of human behaviour, is beginning to play a role in areas such as process control, as well as in mechatronic products combining aspects of electronic, mechanical, and software engineering. Again, the convergence of telecommunications and computing has been a vital factor, allowing the computer to become fully integrated into the manufacturing or other processes (such as computer-integrated manufacturing), thus transcending individual applications such as computer-aided design.

Working practices

The introduction of new technology into areas which have not traditionally used computers has had a great influence on working practices. Some traditional tasks--or even whole categories of tasks--have disappeared completely and new ones have appeared. In some sectors (printing in the UK, for example), adoption of new technology has led to serious industrial conflict.

Once it became commonplace for information retrieval and data processing to be carried out by digital computers in business and industrial settings, it was also natural for such information to be transmitted digitally using a range of new services; telecommunications has therefore become an essential part of many working environments. Small computers are often linked by means of local area networks within an office or company, so that expensive resources such as laser printers or databases can be shared; a further advantage of such networking is that in-house communication can then include electronic mail, computer

17

conferencing, or even voice messaging, as well as the traditional telephone and memo.

Digital telecommunication links extend such facilities to the outside world, providing electronic communication between widely dispersed organizations or individuals, as well as access to external databases or information services. It is even becoming possible for certain employees to work partially or entirely from home, communicating with colleagues via a computer and modem.

In the home, information is available electronically. More recently, with a growth in the ownership of home computers, individual users have linked into the Internet. The combination of telecommunication services (including television), home computer, and new storage media such as videodisc and CD-ROM (compact disc) forms the core of domestic entertainment and educational applications of IT.

Computer architecture

All the above applications of new technology are based upon a computer architecture which has remained virtually unchanged since the early days of the digital computer. Alternative structures such as neural networks are currently arousing much interest, particularly for their potential in artificial-intelligence applications, while parallel computing offers possibilities for faster processing.

In the immediate future, however, further exploitation of new technology is more likely to result from a continuing expansion of telecommunications services and economies of scale in the provision of hardware than from radical changes to computer design. Information technology raises problems of privacy and freedom of information, as data is gathered about citizens who may not have access to records held about them.

18

Computers and Computing

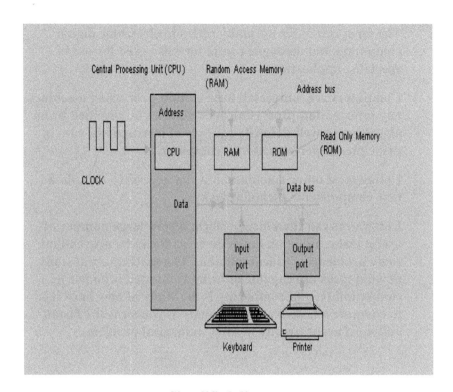

Simplified diagram

When a program is run, the CPU uses the information and instructions in both the ROM and RAM to run the program. The program can send information to the printer or other peripherals.

19

Storing and processing data

A computer is device used for storing and processing data, according to a program of instructions stored within the computer itself.

The term computer normally refers to electronic digital computers, but analogue computers also exist for use in specialist applications.

Computers are 'universal' information-processing machines: any information-processing task that can be specified by an algorithm (a well-defined sequence of instructions) can, in principle, be performed by a computer.

Unlike most other machines, it is not necessary to build a new computer for each new task.

Computers can therefore perform a very large number of useful tasks, although limits do exist: it can be proven that some problems are incomputable. The mathematical study of what tasks are capable of being computed is known as compatibility, and complexity is the study of how hard it is to compute a task. Numerical analysis concerns the fastest and most accurate way to solve numerical problems.

Digital computer

The digital computer is one of the most significant innovations of the 20th century, which leads into the 21st century with significant innovations. In the four decades since its introduction it has had an impact on almost all areas of human activity (under the direction of information technology).

Computers are very widely used commercially for data processing and for information storage and retrieval.

Manufacturing industry has been affected by developments such as computer-integrated manufacture, and robotics.

Much scientific research has been transformed by the ability to analyse large quantities of numerical data and by the use of simulation techniques to model complex systems such as nuclear reactors and the weather. Many technical advances, such as space travel and advanced aircraft design, would have been impossible without the processing ability of computers.

Digital computers are available in a very wide range of powers, sizes, and costs, suitable for different applications. Advances in technology have led to rapid improvements in the performance of all types of computer systems: many personal computers are now more powerful than much larger, mainframe computers of the 1960s.

Computer systems

A computer system can be regarded as being organized in a number of layers. The lowest layer is the hardware (the physical components of the system, as opposed to the software, the programs and other operating information used by the computer).

Both the information which is being processed (the data) and the processing instructions (the program) are stored in the form of bits of information in a memory. The memory unit is connected by a bus to the central processing unit (CPU), which is the other essential hardware component.

The CPU takes one instruction at a time from the memory, decodes it, and then performs the action specified by the instruction. Each instruction specifies a very simple operation, for example, multiplying together two numbers or checking that two pieces of information are identical.

Other hardware items are peripheral devices, which include permanent data storage devices such as hard and floppy disks, input devices for feeding information into the system, and output devices through which results are fed out. A small layer of software above the hardware, called the microcode, allows the computer to execute a larger set of instructions than could be easily provided in hardware alone. The hardware and the microcode together execute machine code.

The next layer in the computer's organization is a much larger body of software, the operating system. It interprets additional, very complex instructions which allow reading from and writing to files, input devices, and output devices.

The layer above this is provided by the compiler or interpreter, which allows a programmer to write programs in a problem-orientated computer language, rather than in machine code or assembly language.

The programmer working with such a language needs to know nothing of the layers below, so that a FORTRAN programmer can regard any computer with a FORTRAN compiler as if it were with a FORTRAN machine.

The final layer of software comprises the computer's applications programs. Computing is about the correct design and implementation of useful applications programs from a given specification. Techniques of software engineering are being developed which make specification, design, and implementation a less error-prone process.

Mathematics and formal reasoning are used to prove logically that the implementation of computer systems correspond to their specifications. Improving the reliability of programs is increasingly important as their use in safety-critical situations grows. Some large computer programs have many millions of instructions, each instruction being a separate 'working part' that must function correctly.

On this basis, computer programs are the most complex artefacts built by humans. The major challenges of computing in the future are the development of software engineering techniques, very high-level computer languages, and parallel processing.

Compact disc

A compact disc (CD) IS a small disc on which audio signals, video signals, or other data can be recorded in digital form (digitization). The disc comprises a clear plastic layer over a reflective aluminium surface. Data is stored on the disc in binary code, the 'ones' of the code being small pits in the plastic surface, the 'zeros' being the smooth plastic. When playing the disc, a laser scans the disc surface: the beam is reflected back only by the 'zero' areas of the disc.

The reflected pulses are picked up by a photo-detector, which converts them into a digital electrical signal. The compact disc was first developed by Philips and Sony in the early 1980s.

By the early 1990s it was the established medium for audio recordings. CD video applies the same technology to videos: discs can be replicated more quickly than videotape and it is easier to access a particular part of the recording. CDs are also used to store large amounts of computer information.

CD-ROM (compact disc with read-only memory) is the most common format, but other forms of disc are available that allow data to be written on to the disc as well as read.

Recent developments are the photo-CD, which records still images on a compact disc for viewing on a television screen or as hard copy, and the multimedia CD, which holds pictures, sound, and text on one CD and plays them back through a television receiver and hi-fi equipment.

Digitisation

Digitisation involves the production of information recorded as a succession of discrete units, rather than as continuously varying (analogue) parameters.

Digital systems most often record information in binary code, using only two states: one and zero. Information such as a message or numerical data can be transmitted from a keyboard by coding the alphabet and other symbols digitally.

A sound may also be recorded (magnetic tape or compact disc) or transmitted in digital form. The electrical signal, into which the sound is converted by a microphone, is analogue in form since the voltage is changing continuously with time, but if the signal is sampled at intervals, then each sample voltage can be coded as a binary number.

For example, a 6-V signal would become 0110, or zero, pulse, pulse, zero. By frequent sampling the whole analogue signal can be represented in a digital form.

Images may also be digitized and held in computer-readable form. In a raster image, the picture is broken up into a rectangular array of pixels, each of which can be represented by a sequence of bits.

There are numerous formats for the files holding raster images. In the simplest, a bit-map format, the file essentially contains sequences of bits, one sequence for each pixel. More commonly, some sort of compression is used.

For example, if a large area of the picture is blue sky of the same colour, it is not necessary to repeat the bit sequence for every picture in this area.

All that is needed is a representation of the correct shade of blue together with an instruction indicating how many times it appears. Photographs and artwork can be digitized using a scanner.

Another type of image file is a vector file. In this, the file contains instructions for drawing and colouring certain shapes; for instance, "draw a rectangle with sides 2 and 3" or "draw a circle with radius 5".

Vector files are not broken into pixels; they are "digitized" in the sense that the information is held in digital form. They are produced by graphics and computer-aided-design (CAD) programs and are generally smaller files than raster-image files.

The digitization of images is particularly important in desktop publishing and electronic publishing.

Artificial Intelligence (AI)

Machines requiring intelligence

Artificial Intelligence (AI) is 'the science of making machines do things that would require intelligence if done by humans' as defined in 1968 by Marvin Minsky of the Massachusetts Institute of Technology, USA.

Sensing, reasoning, pattern recognition, speech recognition, and problem-solving are among such tasks. The degree of sophistication that constitutes AI tends to be revised upwards with each new generation of computers. At its most ambitious level AI has the goal of creating computers and robots capable of reproducing a broad range of human behaviour.

Doubts remain, however, about whether such systems are theoretically or practically possible, because of the vast complexity of the human brain. Unlike the human brain, most computers act serially, one operation at a time. Even supercomputers developed in the 1980s that use 'parallel processing' to carry out billions of operations per second barely begin to match human brain capacity.

Moreover, it has been argued that the brain does not operate using computable algorithms. Experiments in machine translation of natural languages in the 1960s revealed the 'frame problem': most human thought processes use huge amounts of background knowledge or 'context' which it is very difficult to duplicate in a computer.

However, one important result of AI research is the development of systems known as neural networks, which can be 'taught' to solve problems.

These show promise for a number of different AI applications, particularly those involving pattern recognition. The demands of AI have also stimulated the development of computer languages, such as PROLOG and LISP, which are better suited to represent and process symbolic structures than more conventional languages.

Pseudo-Intelligence

'Pseudo-intelligence' is one term for computer applications being developed in translation systems, semi-automatic offices in which human speech and instructions are turned into a properly laid-out document, in linguistic and psycholinguistic studies, and in robotics--replacing human actions by those of a robot, on the production line or in an artificial limb, for example.

Robot sensing is used in weapons guidance systems and in product quality control. The impact of such developments is likely to be huge.

Fifth-generation computer

Most approaches to AI require powerful computer hardware, and it is only since the early 1980s that this has become sufficiently cost-effective to make practical applications possible.

Fifth-generation computers are being developed specifically for use in artificial intelligence. Expert systems were amongst the first AI techniques to be used in practical applications.

Cybernetics

Recently, the term of Cybernetics (from the Greek, *kubernetes*, steersman) has been widely included in the studies of Artificial Intelligence. The term cybernetics was first applied in English by Wiener.

Although cybernetics studies are still (strictly speaking) dedicated the study of communication and control systems in machines, animals, and organizations.

The discipline of cybernetics was developed immediately after World War II, when control-systems and systems-engineering techniques were applied successfully to certain neurological problems.

Cybernetics is characterized by a concentration on the flow of information (rather than energy or material) within a system, and on the use of feedback or 'goal-directed activity' in both technological artefacts and living organisms.

Major areas of cybernetic study have been biological control systems, automation, animal communication, and artificial intelligence (AI).

The recent rapid expansion of AI as a subject area, together with the development of knowledge-based systems and neural networks, have renewed interest in the general cybernetic approach, although the term 'cybernetics' itself is now rarely used.

Robotics

In recent development of Artificial Intelligence, robotics has become part of AI. Although robotics is still considered to be the science and technology of machines designed to function in place of a human being, especially to carry out tasks automatically.

Andreas Sofroniou

The term robot (from the Czech *robota*, 'compulsory service') was coined by the playwright Karel Capek in 1920.

Practical robotics was first formulated by the British inventor C. W. Kenward in 1957, and subsequently exploited in the USA for industrial automation to handle parts for die casting, injection moulding, and metal-cutting machines.

A robot which could manipulate a tool (for painting) was first used in Norway in 1966, and in the USA, robots were developed for spot-welding on assembly lines.

Since then, there has been a continual evolution towards robots of greater precision, such as the Japanese selective *c*ompliance *a*ssembly *r*obot *a*rm (SCARA).

Mechanical manipulator

A modern robot has a mechanical manipulator (usually an arm) and sensors, controlled by a computer. Early hydraulically powered robots have given way to direct-drive machines using electric motors. The main goal of robot research in artificial intelligence is to enable robots to sense and move intelligently around their environment.

Complex tasks

A fifth-generation computer is the term applied to computer systems currently being developed specifically to support artificial intelligence.

In the early 1980s Japan set up a major research project intended to develop the computer hardware and software necessary to perform complex tasks such as machine translation of natural languages, speech recognition, and vision in robotics. Similar projects were also started in the USA and Europe.

The use of artificial intelligence to solve practical problems requires very powerful computers and fifth-generation computers are likely to use more complex computer architectures than conventional computers, involving parallel processing.

In 1991 Japan began a new ten-year research initiative, replacing the fifth-generation programme, to investigate neural networks.

Artificial Intelligence programming languages

In the course of their work on the Logic Theorist and GPS, Newell, Simon, and Shaw developed their Information Processing Language (IPL), a computer language tailored for AI programming. At the heart of IPL was a highly flexible data structure that they called a list.

A list is simply an ordered sequence of items of data. Some or all of the items in a list may themselves be lists. This scheme leads to richly branching structures.

In 1960 John McCarthy combined elements of IPL with the lambda calculus (a formal mathematical-logical system) to produce the programming language LISP (List Processor), which remains the principal language for AI work in the United States.

The lambda calculus itself was invented in 1936 by the Princeton logician Alonzo Church while he was investigating the abstract *Entscheidungsproblem*, or "decision problem," for predicate logic—the same problem that Turing had been attacking when he invented the universal Turing machine.

30

The logic programming language PROLOG (Programmation en Logique) was conceived by Alain Colmerauer at the University of Aix-Marseille, France, where the language was first implemented in 1973.

PROLOG was further developed by the logician Robert Kowalski, a member of the AI group at the University of Edinburgh. This language makes use of a powerful theorem-proving technique known as resolution, invented in 1963 at the U.S. Atomic Energy Commission's Argonne National Laboratory in Illinois by the British logician Alan Robinson.

PROLOG can determine whether or not a given statement follows logically from other given statements. For example, given the statements "All logicians are rational" and "Robinson is a logician," a PROLOG program responds in the affirmative to the query "Robinson is rational?" PROLOG is widely used for AI work, especially in Europe and Japan.

Researchers at the Institute for New Generation Computer Technology in Tokyo have used PROLOG as the basis for sophisticated logic programming languages. Known as fifth-generation languages, these are in use on non-numerical parallel computers developed at the Institute.

Other recent work includes the development of languages for reasoning about time-dependent data such as "the account was paid yesterday." These languages are based on tense logic, which permits statements to be located in the flow of time.

Incidentally, Tense logic was invented in 1953 by the philosopher Arthur Prior at the University of Canterbury, Christchurch, New Zealand.

Expert systems

Expert systems occupy a type of micro-world—for example, a model of a ship's hold and its cargo—that is self-contained and relatively uncomplicated.

For such AI systems every effort is made to incorporate all the information about some narrow field that an expert (or group of experts) would know, so that a good expert system can often outperform any single human expert.

There are many commercial expert systems, including programs for medical diagnosis, chemical analysis, credit authorization, financial management, corporate planning, financial document routing, oil and mineral prospecting, genetic engineering, automobile design and manufacture, camera lens design, computer installation design, airline scheduling, cargo placement, and automatic help services for home computer owners.

Knowledge and inference

The basic components of an expert system are a knowledge base, or KB, and an inference engine. The information to be stored in the KB is obtained by interviewing people who are expert in the area in question.

The interviewer, or knowledge engineer, organizes the information elicited from the experts into a collection of rules, typically of an "if-then" structure. Rules of this type are called production rules. The inference engine enables the expert system to draw deductions from the rules in the knowledge base.

Some expert systems use fuzzy logic. In standard logic there are only two truth values, true and false. This absolute precision makes vague attributes or situations difficult to characterize. (When, precisely, does a thinning head of hair become a bald head?)

Often the rules that human experts use contain vague expressions, and so it is useful for an expert system's inference engine to employ fuzzy logic.

Possible strong Artificial Intelligence

The ongoing success of applied AI and of cognitive simulation seems assured. However, strong AI—that is artificial intelligence that aims to duplicate human intellectual abilities—remains controversial.

Exaggerated claims of success, in professional journals as well as the popular press, have damaged its reputation. At the present time even an embodied system displaying the overall intelligence of a cockroach is proving elusive, let alone a system that can rival a human being.

The difficulty of scaling up AI's modest achievements cannot be overstated. Five decades of research in symbolic AI have failed to produce any firm evidence that a symbol system can manifest human levels of general intelligence; connectionists are unable to model the nervous systems of even the simplest invertebrates; and critics of nouvelle AI regard as simply mystical the view that high-level behaviours involving language understanding, planning, and reasoning will somehow emerge from the interaction of basic behaviours such as obstacle avoidance, gaze control, and object manipulation.

However, this lack of substantial progress may simply be testimony to the difficulty of strong AI, not to its impossibility. Let us turn to the very idea of strong artificial intelligence. Can a computer possibly think? Noam Chomsky suggests that debating this question is pointless, for it is an essentially arbitrary decision whether to extend common usage of the word *think* to include machines.

There is, Chomsky claims, no factual question as to whether any such decision is right or wrong—just as there is no question as to whether our decision to say that airplanes fly is right, or our decision not to say that ships swim is wrong.

However, this seems to oversimplify matters. The important question is, Could it ever be appropriate to say that computers think, and, if so, what conditions must a computer satisfy in order to be so described?

Some authors offer the Turing test as a definition of intelligence. However, Turing himself pointed out that a computer that ought to be described as intelligent might nevertheless fail his test if it were incapable of successfully imitating a human being.

For example, why should an intelligent robot designed to oversee mining on the Moon necessarily be able to pass itself off in conversation as a human being? If an intelligent entity can fail the test, then the test cannot function as a definition of intelligence.

It is even questionable whether passing the test would actually show that a computer is intelligent, as the information theorist Claude Shannon and the AI pioneer John McCarthy pointed out in 1956.

Shannon and McCarthy argued that it is possible, in principle, to design a machine containing a complete set of canned responses to all the questions that an interrogator could possibly ask during the fixed time span of the test.

Like Parry, this machine would produce answers to the interviewer's questions by looking up appropriate responses in a giant table. This objection seems to show that in principle a system with no intelligence at all could pass the Turing test.

In fact, AI has no real definition of intelligence to offer, not even in the subhuman case. Rats are intelligent, but what exactly must an artificial intelligence achieve before researchers can claim this level of success?

In the absence of a reasonably precise criterion for when an artificial system counts as intelligent, there is no objective way of telling whether an AI research program has succeeded or failed.

One result of AI's failure to produce a satisfactory criterion of intelligence is that, whenever researchers achieve one of AI's goals—for example, a program that can summarize newspaper articles or beat the world chess champion— critics are able to say *"That's* not intelligence!"

Marvin Minsky's response to the problem of defining intelligence is to maintain—like Turing before him—that intelligence is simply our name for any problem-solving mental process that we do not yet understand. Minsky likens intelligence to the concept "unexplored regions of Africa": it disappears as soon as we discover it.

Internet

Connecting networks

The term Internet refers to the global network that connects other computer networks, together with software and protocols for controlling the movement of data.

The Internet, often referred to as 'the Net', stems from a network called ARAPNET (Advanced Research Project Agency Network), which was initiated in 1969 by a group of universities and private research groups funded by the US Department of Defense. It now covers almost every country in the world.

Its organization is informal and deliberately non-political--its controllers tend to concentrate on technical aspects rather than on administrative control.

Data access

The Internet offers users a number of basic services including data transfer, electronic mail, and the ability to access information in remote databases. A notable feature is the existence of user groups, which allow people to exchange information and debate specific subjects of interest.

In addition, there are a number of high-level services. For example, MBONE (multicast backbone service) allows the transmission of messages to more than one destination. It is used in videoconferencing.

The World Wide Web, known as 'the Web', is another high-level Internet service, developed in the 1990s at CERN in Geneva. It is a service for distributing multimedia information, including graphics, pictures, sounds, and video as well as text.

A feature of the World Wide Web is that it allows links to other related documents elsewhere on the Internet. Documents for publication on the Web are presented in a form known as HTML (hypertext mark-up language).

This allows a specification of the page layout and typography as it will appear on the screen. It also allows the inclusion of active links to other documents. Generally, these appear on the screen display as highlighted text or as additional icons.

Typically, the user can use a mouse to 'click' on one of these points to load and view a related document. Many commercial and public organizations now have their own Web site (specified by an address code) and publish a 'home page', giving information about the organization.

Early users

Up to the mid-1990s, the major users of the Internet were academic and research organizations. This has begun to change rapidly with individual home users linking in through commercial access providers and with a growing interest by companies in using the Internet for publicity, sales, and as a medium for electronic publishing.

At the same time, there are problems with the flow of information across national borders, bringing in debates about copyright protection, data protection, the publication of pornography, and ultimately political control and censorship.

Internet services

There are various facilities in computers which are also used in the Internet services.

Include are the following:

Networking (in computing) deals with the connecting together of separate computer systems so that they can exchange data, and sometimes programs. The points at which individual systems are connected to the network are known as nodes.

There are two main classes of computer network: broad area (wide area) networks and local area networks (LANs). As the name implies, the nodes of a broad area network may be widely dispersed geographically; in fact the largest networks may extend world-wide.

Typically, broad area networks utilize telecommunication channels to provide the connections between computers.

Local area networks usually link computers or workstations on the same site via coaxial cables or optical fibres. LANs are often used to share expensive peripherals such as laser printers, or to share a central disk store, known as a file server. Both types of network usually provide electronic mail facilities to enable users to pass messages to each other.

Electronic mail

Electronic mail (e-mail) is used for the sending of messages via computer systems. Many computer systems are now connected to local or wide-area networks and users can communicate with other users anywhere on the network.

Some services offer facilities that allow users to send and receive messages via a microcomputer, a telephone, and a modem. The sender and receiver need not be on-line at the time; the message is held in a computer mail-box, which the receiver is able to access.

Electronic publishing

Electronic publishing covers the publication of books, magazines, etc., in electronic form rather than on paper, so that the information is accessible with a computer.

Electronic publications are typically distributed on CD-ROM and generally contain graphics, photographic images, sound, and video clips as well as text (as in multimedia). Publishing on-line is also becoming increasingly important, especially for academic journals.

Currently, a big problem faced by the Internet users is the protection of data, where mal-users deliberately enter false and harmful information. As such, a major new service for the computing users is security, firewalls and the overall facilities for data protection.

Internet architecture

The internet architecture is a system architecture that has revolutionized communications and methods of commerce by allowing various computer networks around the world to interconnect.

Sometimes referred to as a "network of networks," the Internet emerged in the United States in the 1970s but did not become visible to the general public until the early 1990s.

By the beginning of the 21st century, approximately 360 million people, or roughly 6 percent of the world's population, were estimated to have access to the Internet.

39

It is widely assumed that well over one third of the world's population will have some form of Internet access by 2020 and that wireless access will play a growing role.

The Internet provides a capability so powerful and general that it can be used for almost any purpose that depends on information, and it is accessible by every individual who connects to one of its constituent networks.

It supports human communication via electronic mail (e-mail), "chat rooms," newsgroups, and audio and video transmission and allows people to work collaboratively at many different locations. It supports access to digital information by many applications, including the World Wide Web.

The Internet has proven to be a spawning ground for a large and growing number of "e-businesses" (including subsidiaries of traditional "brick-and-mortar" companies) that carry out most of their sales and services over the Internet.

Many experts believe that the Internet has already dramatically transformed business as well as society.

Origin and development

The first computer networks were dedicated special-purpose systems such as SABRE (an airline reservation system) and AUTODIN I (a defence command-and-control system), both designed and implemented in the late 1950s and early 1960s.

By the early 1960s computer manufacturers had begun to use semiconductor technology in commercial products, and both conventional batch-processing and time-sharing systems were in place in many large, technologically advanced companies.

Time-sharing systems allowed a computer's resources to be shared in rapid succession with multiple users, cycling through the queue of users so quickly that the computer appeared dedicated to each user's tasks despite the existence of many others accessing the system "simultaneously." This led to the notion of sharing computer resources (called host computers or simply hosts) over an entire network.

Host-to-host interactions were envisioned, along with access to specialized resources (such as supercomputers and mass storage systems) and interactive access by remote users to the computational powers of time-sharing systems located elsewhere.

These ideas were first realized in ARPANET, which established the first host-to-host network connection on Oct. 29, 1969. It was created by the Advanced Research Projects Agency (ARPA) of the U.S. Department of Defense.

ARPANET was one of the first general-purpose computer networks. It connected time-sharing computers at government-supported research sites, principally universities in the United States, and it soon became a critical piece of infrastructure for the computer science research community in the United States.

Tools and applications—such as the simple mail transfer protocol (SMTP, commonly referred to as e-mail), for sending short messages, and the file transfer protocol (FTP), for longer transmissions—quickly emerged.

In order to achieve cost-effective interactive communications between computers, which typically communicate in short bursts of data, ARPANET employed the new technology of packet switching.

Packet switching takes large messages (or chunks of computer data) and breaks them into smaller, manageable pieces (known as packets) that can travel independently over any available circuit to the target destination, where the pieces are reassembled. Thus, unlike traditional voice communications, packet switching does not require a single dedicated circuit between each pair of users.

Commercial packet networks were introduced in the 1970s, but these were designed principally to provide efficient access to remote computers by dedicated terminals. Briefly, they replaced long-distance modem connections by less-expensive "virtual" circuits over packet networks. In the United States, Telenet and Tymnet were two such packet networks. Neither supported host-to-host communications; in the 1970s this was still the province of the research networks, and it would remain so for many years.

DARPA (Defense Advanced Research Projects Agency; formerly ARPA) supported initiatives for ground-based and satellite-based packet networks.

The ground-based packet radio system provided mobile access to computing resources, while the packet satellite network connected the United States with several European countries and enabled connections with widely dispersed and remote regions. With the introduction of packet radio, connecting a mobile terminal to a computer network became feasible.

However, time-sharing systems were then still too large, unwieldy, and costly to be mobile or even to exist outside a climate-controlled computing environment. A strong motivation thus existed to connect the packet radio network to ARPANET in order to allow mobile users with simple terminals to access the time-sharing systems for which they had authorization.

Similarly, the packet satellite network was used by DARPA to link the United States with satellite terminals serving the United Kingdom, Norway, Germany, and Italy. These terminals, however, had to be connected to other networks

42

in European countries in order to reach the end users. Thus, the need arose to connect the packet satellite net, as well as the packet radio net, with other networks.

Foundation of the Internet

The Internet resulted from the effort to connect various research networks in the United States and Europe. First, DARPA established a program to investigate the interconnection of "heterogeneous networks."

This program, called Inter-netting, was based on the newly introduced concept of open architecture networking, in which networks with defined standard interfaces would be interconnected by "gateways."

A working demonstration of the concept was planned. In order for the concept to work, a new protocol had to be designed and developed; indeed, a system architecture was also required.

In 1974 Vinton Cerf, then at Stanford University in California, and this author, then at DARPA, collaborated on a paper that first described such a protocol and system architecture—namely, the transmission control protocol (TCP), which enabled different types of machines on networks all over the world to route and assemble data packets.

TCP, which originally included the Internet protocol (IP), a global addressing mechanism that allowed routers to get data packets to their ultimate destination, formed the TCP/IP standard, which was adopted by the U.S. Department of Defense in 1980. By the early 1980s the "open architecture" of the TCP/IP approach was adopted and endorsed by many other researchers and eventually by technologists and businessmen around the world.

43

By the 1980s other U.S. governmental bodies were heavily involved with networking, including the National Science Foundation (NSF), the Department of Energy, and the National Aeronautics and Space Administration (NASA). While DARPA had played a seminal role in creating a small-scale version of the Internet among its researchers, NSF worked with DARPA to expand access to the entire scientific and academic community and to make TCP/IP the standard in all federally supported research networks.

In 1985–86 NSF funded the first five supercomputing centres—at Princeton University, the University of Pittsburgh, the University of California, San Diego, the University of Illinois, and Cornell University. In the 1980s NSF also funded the development and operation of the NSFNET, a national "backbone" network to connect these centres.

By the late 1980s the network was operating at millions of bits per second. NSF also funded various non-profit local and regional networks to connect other users to the NSFNET.

A few commercial networks also began in the late 1980s; these were soon joined by others, and the Commercial Internet Exchange (CIX) was formed to allow transit traffic between commercial networks that otherwise would not have been allowed on the NSFNET backbone.

In 1995, after extensive review of the situation, NSF decided that support of the NSFNET infrastructure was no longer required, since many commercial providers were now willing and able to meet the needs of the research community, and its support was withdrawn. Meanwhile, NSF had fostered a competitive collection of commercial Internet backbones connected to one another through so-called network access points (NAPs).

44

From the Internet's origin in the early 1970s, control of it steadily devolved from government stewardship to private-sector participation and finally to private custody with government oversight and forbearance.

Today a loosely structured group of several thousand interested individuals known as the Internet Engineering Task Force participates in a grassroots development process for Internet standards.

Internet standards are maintained by the non-profit Internet Society, an international body with headquarters in Reston, Virginia. The Internet Corporation for Assigned Names and Numbers (ICANN), another non-profit, private organization, oversees various aspects of policy regarding Internet domain names and numbers.

Commercial expansion

The rise of commercial Internet services and applications helped to fuel a rapid commercialization of the Internet.

This phenomenon was the result of several other factors as well. One important factor was the introduction of the personal computer and the workstation in the early 1980s— a development that in turn was fuelled by unprecedented progress in integrated circuit technology and an attendant rapid decline in computer prices.

Another factor, which took on increasing importance, was the emergence of Ethernet and other "local area networks" to link personal computers. But other forces were at work too.

Following the restructuring of AT&T in 1984, NSF took advantage of various new options for national-level digital backbone services for the NSFNET. In 1988 the Corporation

45

for National Research Initiatives received approval to conduct an experiment linking a commercial e-mail service (MCI Mail) to the Internet.

This application was the first Internet connection to a commercial provider that was not also part of the research community. Approval quickly followed to allow other e-mail providers access, and the Internet began its first explosion in traffic.

In 1993 federal legislation allowed NSF to open the NSFNET backbone to commercial users. Prior to that time, use of the backbone was subject to an "acceptable use" policy, established and administered by NSF, under which commercial use was limited to those applications that served the research community.

NSF recognized that commercially supplied network services, now that they were available, would ultimately be far less expensive than continued funding of special-purpose network services.

Also in 1993 the University of Illinois made widely available Mosaic, a new type of computer program, known as a browser, that ran on most types of computers and, through its "point-and-click" interface, simplified access, retrieval, and display of files through the Internet.

Mosaic incorporated a set of access protocols and display standards originally developed at the European Organization for Nuclear Research (CERN) by Tim Berners-Lee for a new Internet application called the World Wide Web (WWW).

In 1994 Netscape Communications Corporation (originally called Mosaic Communications Corporation) was formed to further develop the Mosaic browser and server software for commercial use. Shortly thereafter, the software giant Microsoft Corporation became interested in supporting

Internet applications on personal computers (PCs) and developed its Internet Explorer Web browser (based initially on Mosaic) and other programs.

These new commercial capabilities accelerated the growth of the Internet, which as early as 1988 had already been growing at the rate of 100 percent per year.

By the late 1990s there were approximately 10,000 Internet service providers (ISPs) around the world, more than half located in the United States.

However, most of these ISPs provided only local service and relied on access to regional and national ISPs for wider connectivity. Consolidation began at the end of the decade, with many small to medium-size providers merging or being acquired by larger ISPs.

Among these larger providers were groups such as America Online, Inc. (AOL), which started as a dial-up information service with no Internet connectivity but made a transition in the late 1990s to become the leading provider of Internet services in the world—with more than 25 million subscribers by 2000 and with branches in Australia, Europe, South America, and Asia.

Widely used Internet "portals" such as AOL, Yahoo!, Excite, and others were able to command advertising fees owing to the number of "eyeballs" that visited their sites. Indeed, during the late 1990s advertising revenue became the main quest of many Internet sites, some of which began to speculate by offering free or low-cost services of various kinds that were visually augmented with advertisements.

By 2001 this speculative bubble had burst.

Future directions

While the precise structure of the future Internet is not yet clear, many directions of growth seem apparent. One is the increased availability of wireless access. Wireless services enable applications not previously possible in any economical fashion.

For example, global positioning systems (GPS) combined with wireless Internet access would help mobile users to locate alternate routes, generate precise accident reports and initiate recovery services, and improve traffic management and congestion control. In addition to wireless laptop computers and personal digital assistants (PDAs), wearable devices with voice input and special display glasses are under development.

Another future direction is toward higher backbone and network access speeds. Remaining bandwidth could be used to transmit auxiliary information about the data being sent, which in turn would enable rapid customization of displays and prompt resolution of certain local queries.

Much research, both public and private, has gone into integrated broadband systems that can simultaneously carry multiple signals—data, voice, and video. In particular, the U.S. government has funded research to create new high-speed network capabilities dedicated to the scientific-research community.

It is clear that communications connectivity will be an important function of a future Internet as more machines and devices are interconnected.

In 1998, after four years of study, the Internet Engineering Task Force published a new 128-bit IP address standard intended to replace the conventional 32-bit standard.

The dissemination of digitised text, pictures, and audio and video recordings over the Internet, primarily available today through the World Wide Web, has resulted in an information explosion.

Clearly, powerful tools are needed to manage network-based information.

Information available on the Internet today may not be available tomorrow without careful attention being paid to preservation and archiving techniques. The key to making information persistently available is infrastructure and the management of that infrastructure.

Repositories of information, stored as digital objects, will soon populate the Internet. At first these repositories may be dominated by digital objects specifically created and formatted for the World Wide Web, but in time they will contain objects of all kinds in formats that will be dynamically resolvable by users' computers in real time.

Movement of digital objects from one repository to another will still leave them available to users who are authorized to access them, while replicated instances of objects in multiple repositories will provide alternatives to users who are better able to interact with certain parts of the Internet than with others. Information will have its own identity and, indeed, become a "first-class citizen" on the Internet.

Society and the Internet

What began as a largely technical and limited universe of designers and users became one of the most important mediums of the late 20th and early 21st centuries. As the Pew Charitable Trust observed in 2004, it took 46 years to wire 30 percent of the United States for electricity; it took only 7 years for the Internet to reach that same level of connection to American homes. By 2005, 68 percent of American adults and 90 percent of American teenagers had used the Internet. Europe and Asia were at least as well connected as the United States.

Nearly half of the citizens of the European Union are online, and even higher rates are found in the Scandinavian countries. There is a wide variance in Asian countries; for example, by 2005 Taiwan, Hong Kong, and Japan had at least half of their populations online, whereas India, Pakistan, and Vietnam had less than 10 percent.

South Korea was the world leader in connecting its population to the Internet through high-speed broadband connections.

Such statistics can chart the Internet's growth, but they offer few insights into the changes wrought as users—individuals, groups, corporations, and governments—have embedded the technology into everyday life.

The Internet is now as much a lived experience as a tool for performing particular tasks, offering the possibility of creating an environment or virtual reality in which individuals might work, socially interact with others, and perhaps even live out their lives.

Data protection

Data protection, therefore, covers the necessary arrangements, thus ensuring that confidential information, and especially computerized information, is available only to people entitled to use it.

The twin purposes are to maintain the confidentiality of personal information and business secrets, and to enable the subjects on whom information is stored to ensure its accuracy.

Electronic methods for combating unauthorized access to computers are supplemented in many countries by legal requirements.

Typically, people who hold information about others are obliged to register with a regulatory agency, to comply with its codes of practice and to permit individuals to check and correct their records. Wrongfully obtaining access to material may be a criminal offence.

Databases

Related data

A database is a logically organized collection of related data, generally accessed by a set of programs known as a database management system (DBMS), which oversees the creation and use of the database and controls access to the data.

The organization of a database obviates the need to duplicate information to meet the various requirements of different groups of users, and ensures that the data always remains consistent.

A large database requires extensive storage facilities. In some organizations and services databases can be accessed over networks from microcomputers or as videotex. 'Relational' databases and hypertext techniques include extensive and complex cross-reference facilities so that information on related items may be retrieved.

Many database programs have been designed to run on micro-computers. Some of these contain computer languages that enable users to change the operation of the database to suit their requirements.

For example, a mailing list on a micro-computer constitutes a simple database in which--if the information were available in a structured format--the DBMS could be instructed to print out the addresses of all the people called Smith, or of everyone on the mailing list living in Melbourne, Australia.

Data in formats

Data (computing) is information that has been prepared, often in a particular format, for a specific purpose.

In computing, the term data is used for material distinct from instructions: for example, if a computer multiplies two numbers together, the numbers themselves are the data, operated on by an instruction (to multiply them together).

In a more restricted sense, data may be the information input for a particular program, as opposed to the results or output.

A third meaning uses data as a term for information not in the form of words, sounds, or images: such data is usually information that is stored in a highly organized and compact form suitable for data processing.

Processing of data

Data processing refers to the use of a computer to manipulate data, particularly the routine tasks undertaken in large organizations. For example, the maintenance, retrieval, and analysis of financial records is faster and easier with the aid of computers.

The amount of data which needs to be processed is frequently considerable. Therefore, the data is often organized in the form of a single database.

The database is stored on hard disks, magnetic drums, or magnetic tapes attached to computers of substantial power. Large data-processing facilities are often distributed over networks in which a user anywhere on the network can access data anywhere else on the network.

Storage of files

A database is stored as a file or a set of files on magnetic disk or tape, optical disk, or some other secondary storage device.

The information in these files may be broken down into records, each of which consists of one or more fields. Fields are the basic units of data storage and each field typically contains information pertaining to one aspect or attribute of the entity described by the database.

Records are also organized into tables that include information about relationships between its various fields. Although database is applied loosely to any collection of information in computer files, a database in the strict sense provides cross-referencing capabilities.

Using keywords and various sorting commands, users can rapidly search, rearrange, group, and select the fields in many records to retrieve or create reports on particular aggregates of data.

Database records and files must be organized to allow retrieval of the information. Queries are the main way users retrieve database information. The power of a DBMS comes from its ability to define new relationships from the basic ones given by the tables and to use them to get responses to queries.

Typically, the user provides a string of characters, and the computer searches the database for a corresponding sequence and provides the source materials in which those characters appear; a user can request, for example, all records in which the contents of the field for a person's last name is the word Smith.

The many users of a large database must be able to manipulate the information within it quickly at any given time. Moreover, large business and other organizations tend

54

to build up many independent files containing related and even overlapping data, and their data-processing activities often require the linking of data from several files.

Several different types of DBMS have been developed to support these requirements: flat, hierarchical, network, relational, and object-oriented.

Early systems were arranged sequentially (i.e., alphabetically, numerically, or chronologically); the development of direct-access storage devices made possible random access to data via indexes.

In flat databases, records are organized according to a simple list of entities; many simple databases for personal computers are flat in structure.

The records in hierarchical databases are organized in a treelike structure, with each level of records branching off into a set of smaller categories.

Unlike hierarchical databases, which provide single links between sets of records at different levels, network databases create multiple linkages between sets by placing links, or pointers, to one set of records in another; the speed and versatility of network databases have led to their wide use within businesses and in e-commerce.

Relational databases are used where associations between files or records cannot be expressed by links; a simple flat list becomes one row of a table, or "relation," and multiple relations can be mathematically associated to yield desired information. Various iterations of SQL (Structured Query Language) are widely employed in DBMS for relational databases.

Object-oriented databases store and manipulate more complex data structures, called "objects," which are organized into hierarchical classes that may inherit properties from classes higher in the chain; this database structure is the most flexible and adaptable.

The information in many databases consists of natural-language texts of documents; number-oriented databases primarily contain information such as statistics, tables, financial data, and raw scientific and technical data. Small databases can be maintained on personal-computer systems and may be used by individuals at home.

These and larger databases have become increasingly important in business life, in part because they are now commonly designed to be integrated with other office software, including spreadsheet programs.

Typical commercial database applications include airline reservations, production management functions, medical records in hospitals, and legal records of insurance companies.

The largest databases are usually maintained by governmental agencies, business organizations, and universities. These databases may contain texts of such materials as abstracts, reports, legal statutes, wire services, newspapers and journals, encyclopaedias, and catalogs of various kinds.

Reference databases contain bibliographies or indexes that serve as guides to the location of information in books, periodicals, and other published literature.

Thousands of these publicly accessible databases now exist, covering topics ranging from law, medicine, and engineering to news and current events, games, classified advertisements, and instructional courses.

Increasingly, formerly separate databases are being combined electronically into larger collections known as data warehouses.

Businesses and government agencies then employ "data mining" software to analyze multiple aspects of the data for various patterns.

For example, a government agency might flag for human investigation a company or individual that purchased a suspicious quantity of certain equipment or materials, even though the purchases were spread around the country or through various subsidiaries.

Data-mining approaches

The complete data-mining process involves multiple steps, from understanding the goals of a project and what data are available to implementing process changes based on the final analysis. The three key computational steps are the model-learning process, model evaluation, and use of the model.

This division is clearest with classification of data. Model learning occurs when one algorithm is applied to data about which the group (or class) attribute is known in order to produce a classifier, or an algorithm learned from the data.

The classifier is then tested with an independent evaluation set that contains data with known attributes. The extent to which the model's classifications agree with the known class for the target attribute can then be used to determine the expected accuracy of the model. If the model is sufficiently accurate, it can be used to classify data for which the target attribute is unknown.

57

Data-mining techniques

There are many types of data mining, typically divided by the kind of information (attributes) known and the type of knowledge sought from the data-mining model.

Predictive modelling

Predictive modelling is used when the goal is to estimate the value of a particular target attribute and there exist sample training data for which values of that attribute are known.

An example is classification, which takes a set of data already divided into predefined groups and searches for patterns in the data that differentiate those groups. These discovered patterns then can be used to classify other data where the right group designation for the target attribute is unknown (though other attributes may be known).

For instance, a manufacturer could develop a predictive model that distinguishes parts that fail under extreme heat, extreme cold, or other conditions based on their manufacturing environment, and this model may then be used to determine appropriate applications for each part.

Another technique employed in predictive modelling is regression analysis, which can be used when the target attribute is a numeric value and the goal is to predict that value for new data.

Descriptive modelling

Descriptive modelling, or clustering, also divides data into groups. With clustering, however, the proper groups are not

58

known in advance; the patterns discovered by analyzing the data are used to determine the groups.

For example, an advertiser could analyze a general population in order to classify potential customers into different clusters and then develop separate advertising campaigns targeted to each group.

Fraud detection also makes use of clustering to identify groups of individuals with similar purchasing patterns.

Pattern mining

Pattern mining concentrates on identifying rules that describe specific patterns within the data.

Market-basket analysis, which identifies items that typically occur together in purchase transactions, was one of the first applications of data mining.

For example, supermarkets used market-basket analysis to identify items that were often purchased together—for instance, a store featuring a fish sale would also stock up on tartar sauce.

Although testing for such associations has long been feasible and is often simple to see in small data sets, data mining has enabled the discovery of less apparent associations in immense data sets. Of most interest is the discovery of unexpected associations, which may open new avenues for marketing or research.

Another important use of pattern mining is the discovery of sequential patterns; for example, sequences of errors or warnings that precede an equipment failure may be used to schedule preventative maintenance or may provide insight into a design flaw.

59

Anomaly detection

Anomaly detection can be viewed as the flip side of clustering—that is, finding data instances that are unusual and do not fit any established pattern. Fraud detection is an example of anomaly detection.

Although fraud detection may be viewed as a problem for predictive modelling, the relative rarity of fraudulent transactions and the speed with which criminals develop new types of fraud mean that any predictive model is likely to be of low accuracy and to quickly become out of date.

Thus, anomaly detection instead concentrates on modelling what is normal behaviour in order to identify unusual transactions. Anomaly detection also is used with various monitoring systems, such as for intrusion detection.

Numerous other data-mining techniques have been developed, including pattern discovery in time series data (e.g., stock prices), streaming data (e.g., sensor networks), and relational learning (e.g., social networks).

Concerns and future directions

The potential for invasion of privacy using data mining has been a concern for many people.

Commercial databases may contain detailed records of people's medical history, purchase transactions, and telephone usage, among other aspects of their lives.

Civil libertarians consider some databases held by businesses and governments to be an unwarranted intrusion and an invitation to abuse.

For example, the American Civil Liberties Union sued the U.S. National Security Agency (NSA) alleging warrant-less spying on American citizens through the acquisition of call records from some American telecommunication companies.

The program, which began in 2001, was not discovered by the public until 2006, when the information began to leak out.

Often the risk is not from data mining itself (which usually aims to produce general knowledge rather than to learn information about specific issues) but from misuse or inappropriate disclosure of information in these databases.

In the United States, many federal agencies are now required to produce annual reports that specifically address the privacy implications of their data-mining projects. The U.S. law requiring privacy reports from federal agencies defines data mining quite restrictively as "...analyses to discover or locate a predictive pattern or anomaly indicative of terrorist or criminal activity on the part of any individual or individuals."

As various local, national, and international law-enforcement agencies have begun to share or integrate their databases, the potential for abuse or security breaches has forced governments to work with industry on developing more secure computers and networks.

In particular, there has been research in techniques for privacy-preserving data mining that operate on distorted, transformed, or encrypted data to decrease the risk of disclosure of any individual's data.

Data mining is evolving, with one driver being competitions on challenge problems. A commercial example of this was the $1 million Netflix Prize. Netflix, an American company that offers movie rentals delivered by mail or streamed over the Internet, began the contest in 2006 to see if anyone could improve by 10 percent its recommendation system, an algorithm for predicting an individual's movie preferences based on previous rental data.

The prize was awarded on Sept. 21, 2009, to BellKor's Pragmatic Chaos—a team of seven mathematicians, computer scientists, and engineers from the United States, Canada, Austria, and Israel who had achieved the 10 percent goal on June 26, 2009, and finalized their victory with an improved algorithm 30 days later.

The three-year open competition had spurred many clever data-mining innovations from contestants. For example, the 2007 and 2008 Conferences on Knowledge Discovery and Data Mining held workshops on the Netflix Prize, at which research papers were presented on topics ranging from new collaborative filtering techniques to faster matrix factorization (a key component of many recommendation systems). Concerns over privacy of such data have also led to advances in understanding privacy and anonymity.

Data mining is not a panacea, however, and results must be viewed with the same care as with any statistical analysis. One of the strengths of data mining is the ability to analyze quantities of data that would be impractical to analyze manually, and the patterns found may be complex and difficult for humans to understand; this complexity requires care in evaluating the patterns.

Nevertheless, statistical evaluation techniques can result in knowledge that is free from human bias, and the large amount of data can reduce biases inherent in smaller samples. Used properly, data mining provides valuable insights into large data sets that otherwise would not be practical or possible to obtain.

Networking

Network (in computing) is used for the connecting together of separate computer systems so that they can exchange data, and sometimes programs.

The points at which individual systems are connected to the network are known as nodes. There are two main classes of computer network: broad area (wide area) networks and local area networks (LANs). As the name implies, the nodes of a broad area network may be widely dispersed geographically; in fact the largest networks may extend world-wide.

Typically, broad area networks utilize telecommunication channels to provide the connections between computers. Local area networks usually link computers or workstations on the same site via coaxial cables or optical fibres. LANs are often used to share expensive peripherals such as laser printers, or to share a central disk store, known as a file server. Both types of network usually provide electronic mail facilities to enable users to pass messages to each other.

Hypertext

Hypertext is a generic term for computer systems used to store, retrieve, and view multidimensional documents. Hypertext systems are more flexible than conventional databases.

Links may be made between parts of a hypertext document so that it can be read in a non-standard order, when pursuing a particular topic. Viewed text may be selected by using a mouse or keyboard, and displayed in a window. The first practical hypertext systems were developed in the 1980s, and are particularly suited to multimedia applications.

63

Systems protection

This is a continuous development of software and hardware devices for the protection of computer systems and information from harm, theft, and unauthorized use.

Computer hardware is typically protected by the same means used to protect other valuable or sensitive equipment, namely, serial numbers, doors and locks, and alarms.

The protection of information and system access, on the other hand, is achieved through other tactics, some of them quite complex.

The security precautions related to computer information and access address four major threats:

(1) Theft of data, such as that of military secrets from government computers;

(2) Vandalism, including the destruction of data by a computer virus;

(3) Fraud, such as employees at a bank channelling funds into their own accounts; and

(4) Invasion of privacy, such as the illegal accessing of protected personal financial or medical data from a large database.

The most basic means of protecting a computer system against theft, vandalism, invasion of privacy, and other irresponsible behaviours is to electronically track and record the access to, and activities of, the various users of a computer system.

This is commonly done by assigning an individual password to each person who has access to a system. The computer system itself can then automatically track the use of these passwords, recording such data as which files were accessed under particular passwords and so on. Another security measure is to store a system's data on a separate device, or medium, such as magnetic tape or disks, that is normally inaccessible through the computer system. Finally, data is often encrypted so that it can be deciphered only by holders of a singular encryption key.

Computer security has become increasingly important since the late 1960s, when modems (devices that allow computers to communicate over telephone lines) were introduced. The proliferation of personal computers in the 1980s compounded the problem because they enabled hackers (irresponsible computerphiles) to illegally access major computer systems from the privacy of their homes.

The development of advanced security techniques continues to diminish such threats, though concurrent refinements in the methods of computer crime pose ongoing hazards.

Computer crime

The computer crime involves the use of a computer as an instrument to further illegal ends, such as committing fraud, trafficking in child pornography and intellectual property, stealing identities, or violating privacy.

Cyber crime, especially through the Internet, has grown in importance as the computer has become central to commerce, entertainment, and government. Because of the early and widespread adoption of computers and the Internet in the United States, most of the earliest victims and villains of cyber crime were Americans.

By the 21st century, though, hardly a hamlet remained anywhere in the world that had not been touched by cyber crime of one sort or another.

Cyber crime

Defining cyber crime

New technologies create new criminal opportunities but few new types of crime. What distinguishes cyber crime from traditional criminal activity? Obviously, one difference is the use of the digital computer, but technology alone is insufficient for any distinction that might exist between different realms of criminal activity.

Criminals do not need a computer to commit fraud, traffic in child pornography and intellectual property, steal an identity, or violate someone's privacy. All those activities existed before the "cyber" prefix became ubiquitous. Cyber crime, especially involving the Internet, represents an extension of existing criminal behaviour alongside some novel illegal activities.

Most cyber crime is an attack on information about individuals, corporations, or governments. Although the attacks do not take place on a physical body, they do take place on the personal or corporate virtual body, which is the set of informational attributes that define people and institutions on the Internet.

In other words, in the digital age our virtual identities are essential elements of everyday life: we are a bundle of numbers and identifiers in multiple computer databases owned by governments and corporations.

Cyber crime highlights the centrality of networked computers in our lives, as well as the fragility of such seemingly solid facts as individual identity.

An important aspect of cyber crime is its non-local character: actions can occur in jurisdictions separated by

Andreas Sofroniou

vast distances. This poses severe problems for law enforcement since previously local or even national crimes now require international cooperation.

For example, if a person accesses child pornography located on a computer in a country that does not ban child pornography, is that individual committing a crime in a nation where such materials are illegal? Where exactly does cyber crime take place? Cyberspace is simply a richer version of the space where a telephone conversation takes place, somewhere between the two people having the conversation.

As a planet-spanning network, the Internet offers criminals multiple hiding places in the real world as well as in the network itself.

However, just as individuals walking on the ground leave marks that a skilled tracker can follow, cyber criminals leave clues as to their identity and location, despite their best efforts to cover their tracks. In order to follow such clues across national boundaries, though, international cyber-crime treaties must be ratified.

In 1996 the Council of Europe, together with government representatives from the United States, Canada, and Japan, drafted a preliminary international treaty covering computer crime.

Around the world, civil libertarian groups immediately protested provisions in the treaty requiring Internet service providers (ISPs) to store information on their customers' transactions and to turn this information over on demand. Work on the treaty proceeded nevertheless, and on November 23, 2001, the Council of Europe Cyber-crime Convention was signed by 30 states.

Additional protocols, covering terrorist activities and racist and xenophobic cyber crimes, were proposed in 2002. In addition, various national laws, such as the USA PATRIOT Act of 2001, have expanded law enforcement's power to monitor and protect computer networks.

Types of cyber crime

Cyber-crime ranges across a spectrum of activities. At one end are crimes that involve fundamental breaches of personal or corporate privacy, such as assaults on the integrity of information held in digital depositories and the use of illegally obtained digital information to blackmail a firm or individual. Also at this end of the spectrum is the growing crime of identity theft.

Midway along the spectrum lie transaction-based crimes such as fraud, trafficking in child pornography, digital piracy, money laundering, and counterfeiting. These are specific crimes with specific victims, but the criminal hides in the relative anonymity provided by the Internet.

Another part of this type of crime involves individuals within corporations or government bureaucracies deliberately altering data for either profit or political objectives. At the other end of the spectrum are those crimes that involve attempts to disrupt the actual workings of the Internet.

These range from spam, hacking, and denial of service attacks against specific sites to acts of cyberterrorism—that is, the use of the Internet to cause public disturbances and even death.

Cyber-terrorism focuses upon the use of the Internet by non-state actors to affect a nation's economic and technological infrastructure. Since the September 11 attacks of 2001, public awareness of the threat of cyber-terrorism has grown dramatically.

Identity theft

Cyber-crime affects both a virtual and a real body, but the effects upon each are different. This phenomenon is clearest in the case of identity theft.

In the United States, for example, individuals do not have an official identity card but a Social Security number that has long served as a de facto identification number.

Taxes are collected on the basis of each citizen's Social Security number, and many private institutions use the number to keep track of their employees, students, and patients.

Access to an individual's Social Security number affords the opportunity to gather all the documents related to that person's citizenship—i.e., to steal his identity.

Even stolen credit card information can be used to reconstruct an individual's identity. When criminals steal a firm's credit card records, they produce two distinct effects.

First, they make off with digital information about individuals that is useful in many ways. For example, they might use the credit card information to run up huge bills, forcing the credit card firms to suffer large losses, or they might sell the information to others who can use it in a similar fashion.

Second, they might use individual credit card names and numbers to create new identities for other criminals. For example, a criminal might contact the issuing bank of a stolen credit card and change the mailing address on the account.

Next, the criminal may get a passport or driver's license with his own picture but with the victim's name. With a driver's license, the criminal can easily acquire a new Social Security card; it is then possible to open bank accounts and receive loans—all with the victim's credit record and background.

The original cardholder might remain unaware of this until the debt is so great that the bank contacts the account holder. Only then does the identity theft become visible.

Although identity theft takes places in many countries, researchers and law-enforcement officials are plagued by a lack of information and statistics about the crime worldwide.

Interpol, the international policing agency, has not added any type of cyber-crime, including identity theft, to its annual crime statistics. Cyber-crime is clearly, however, an international problem.

Internet fraud

Schemes to defraud consumers abound on the Internet. Among the most famous is the Nigerian, or "419," scam; the number is a reference to the section of Nigerian law that the scam violates.

Although this con has been used with both fax and traditional mail, it has been given new life by the Internet. In the scheme, an individual receives an e-mail asserting that the sender requires help in transferring a large sum of money out of Nigeria or another distant country.

Usually, this money is in the form of an asset that is going to be sold, such as oil, or a large amount of cash that requires "laundering" to conceal its source; the variations are endless, and new specifics are constantly being developed.

The message asks the recipient to cover some cost of moving the funds out of the country in return for receiving a much larger sum of money in the near future. Should the recipient respond with a check or money order, he is told that complications have developed; more money is required.

Over time, victims can lose thousands of dollars that are utterly unrecoverable.

Despite a vast amount of consumer education, Internet fraud remains a growth industry for criminals and prosecutors. Europe and the United States are far from the only sites of cyber crime. South Korea is among the most wired countries in the world, and its cyber-crime fraud statistics are growing at an alarming rate. Japan has also experienced a rapid growth in similar crimes.

Automated teller machine fraud

Computers also make more mundane types of fraud possible. Take the automated teller machine (ATM) through which many people now get cash. In order to access an account, a user supplies a card and personal identification number (PIN).

Criminals have developed means to intercept both the data on the card's magnetic strip as well as the user's PIN. In turn, the information is used to create fake cards that are then used to withdraw funds from the unsuspecting individual's account. For example, in 2002 the *New York Times* reported that more than 21,000 American bank accounts had been skimmed by a single group engaged in acquiring ATM information illegally.

A particularly effective form of fraud has involved the use of ATMs in shopping centres and convenience stores. These machines are free-standing and not physically part of a bank.

71

Criminals can easily set up a machine that looks like a legitimate machine; instead of dispensing money, however, the machine gathers information on users and only tells them that the machine is out of order after they have typed in their PINs. Given that ATMs are the preferred method for dispensing currency all over the world, ATM fraud has become an international problem.

Wire fraud

The international nature of cyber-crime is particularly evident with wire fraud. One of the largest and best-organized wire fraud schemes was orchestrated by Vladimir Levin, a Russian programmer with a computer software firm in St. Petersburg. In 1994, with the aid of dozens of confederates, Levin began transferring some $10 million from subsidiaries of Citibank, N.A., in Argentina and Indonesia to bank accounts in San Francisco, Tel Aviv, Amsterdam, Germany, and Finland.

According to Citibank, all but $400,000 was eventually recovered as Levin's accomplices attempted to withdraw the funds. Levin himself was arrested in 1995 while in transit through London's Heathrow Airport (at the time, Russia had no extradition treaty for cyber crime). In 1998 Levin was finally extradited to the United States, where he was sentenced to three years in jail and ordered to reimburse Citibank $240,015.

Exactly how Levin obtained the necessary account names and passwords has never been disclosed, but no Citibank employee has ever been charged in connection with the case.

Because a sense of security and privacy are paramount to financial institutions, the exact extent of wire fraud is difficult to ascertain.

In the early 21st century, wire fraud remained a worldwide problem.

Piracy

Sales of compact discs (CDs) are the major source of revenue for recording companies. Although piracy—that is, the illegal duplication of copyrighted materials—has always been a problem, especially in the Far East, the proliferation on college campuses of inexpensive personal computers capable of capturing music off CDs and sharing them over high-speed ("broadband") Internet connections has become the recording industry's greatest nightmare.

In the United States, the recording industry, represented by the Recording Industry Association of America (RIAA), attacked a single file-sharing service, Napster, which from 1999 to 2001 allowed users across the Internet access to music files, stored in the data-compression format known as MP3, on other users' computers by way of Napster's central computer.

According to the RIAA, Napster users regularly violated the copyright of recording artists, and the service had to stop. For users, the issues were not so clear-cut. At the core of the Napster case was the issue of fair use. Individuals who had purchased a CD were clearly allowed to listen to the music, whether in their home stereo, automobile sound system, or personal computer.

What they did not have the right to do, argued the RIAA, was to make the CD available to thousands of others who could make a perfect digital copy of the music and create their own CDs.

Users rejoined that sharing their files was a fair use of copyrighted material for which they had paid a fair price. In the end, the RIAA argued that a whole new class of cyber criminal had been born—the digital pirate—that included just about anyone who had ever shared or downloaded an MP3 file.

Although the RIAA successfully shuttered Napster, a new type of file-sharing service, known as peer-to-peer (P2P) networks, sprang up. These decentralized systems do not rely on a central facilitating computer; instead, they consist of millions of users who voluntarily open their own computers to others for file sharing.

The RIAA continues to battle these file-sharing networks, demanding that ISPs turn over records of their customers who move large quantities of data over their networks, but the effects have been minimal.

The RIAA's other tactic has been to push for the development of technologies to enforce the digital rights of copyright holders. So-called digital rights management (DRM) technology is an attempt to forestall piracy through technologies that will not allow consumers to share files or possess "too many" copies of a copyrighted work.

As companies work on the hardware and software necessary to meet these goals, it is clear that file sharing has brought about a fundamental reconstruction of the relationship between producers, distributors, and consumers of artistic material.

As broadband Internet connections proliferate, the motion-picture industry faces a similar problem, although the digital videodisc (DVD) came to market with encryption and various built-in attempts to avoid the problems of a video Napster.

At the start of the 21st century, copyright owners began accommodating themselves with the idea of commercial digital distribution. Examples include the online sales by the iTunes Store (run by Apple Inc.) and Amazon.com of music, television shows, and movies in downloadable formats, with and without DRM restrictions.

In addition, several cable and satellite television providers, as well as many electronic game systems (Sony Corporation's PlayStation 3 and Microsoft Corporation's Xbox 360), have developed "video-on-demand" services that allow customers to download movies and shows for immediate (streaming) or later playback.

Forgery

File sharing of intellectual property is only one aspect of the problem with copies. Another more mundane aspect lies in the ability of digital devices to render nearly perfect copies of material artefacts. Take the traditional crime of counterfeiting.

Until recently, creating passable currency required a significant amount of skill and access to technologies that individuals usually do not own, such as printing presses, engraving plates, and special inks.

The advent of inexpensive, high-quality colour copiers and printers has brought counterfeiting to the masses. Ink-jet printers now account for a growing percentage of the counterfeit currency confiscated by the U.S. Secret Service. In 1995 ink-jet currency accounted for 0.5 percent of counterfeit U.S. currency; in 1997 ink-jet printers produced 19 percent of the illegal cash.

The widespread development and use of computer technology prompted the U.S. Treasury to redesign U.S. paper currency to include a variety of anti-counterfeiting technologies.

The European Union currency, or euro, had security designed into it from the start. Special features, such as embossed foil holograms and special ribbons and paper, were designed to make counterfeiting difficult.

Indeed, the switch to the euro presented an unprecedented opportunity for counterfeiters of pre-existing national currencies. The great fear was that counterfeit currency would be laundered into legal euros. Fortunately, it was not the problem that some believed it would be.

Child pornography

With the advent of almost every new media technology, pornography has been its "killer app," or the application that drove early deployment of technical innovations in search of profit.

The Internet was no exception, but there is a criminal element to this business bonanza—child pornography, which is unrelated to the lucrative business of legal adult-oriented pornography.

The possession of child pornography, defined here as images of children under age 18 engaged in sexual behaviour, is illegal in the United States, the European Union, and many other countries, but it remains a problem that has no easy solution.

The problem is compounded by the ability of "kiddie porn" Web sites to disseminate their material from locations, such as states of the former Soviet Union as well as Southeast Asia, that lack cyber-crime laws.

Some law-enforcement organizations believe that child pornography represents a $3-billion-a-year industry and that more than 10,000 Internet locations provide access to these materials.

The Internet also provides pedophiles with an unprecedented opportunity to commit criminal acts through the use of "chat rooms" to identify and lure victims. Here the virtual and the material worlds intersect in a particularly dangerous fashion.

In many countries, state authorities now pose as children in chat rooms; despite the widespread knowledge of this practice, pedophiles continue to make contact with these "children" in order to meet them "off-line." That such a meeting invites a high risk of immediate arrest does not seem to deter pedophiles.

Interestingly enough, it is because the Internet allows individual privacy to be breached that the authorities are able to capture pedophiles.

Hacking

While breaching privacy to detect cyber crime works well when the crimes involve the theft and misuse of information, ranging from credit card numbers and personal data to file sharing of various commodities—music, video, or child pornography—what of crimes that attempt to wreak havoc on the very workings of the machines that make up the network?

The story of hacking actually goes back to the 1950s, when a group of phreaks (short for "phone freaks") began to hijack portions of the world's telephone networks, making unauthorized long-distance calls and setting up special "party lines" for fellow phreaks.

With the proliferation of computer bulletin board systems (BBSs) in the late 1970s, the informal phreaking culture began to coalesce into quasi-organized groups of individuals who graduated from the telephone network to "hacking" corporate and government computer network systems.

Although the term *hacker* predates computers and was used as early as the mid-1950s in connection with electronic hobbyists, the first recorded instance of its use in connection with computer programmers who were adept at writing, or "hacking," computer code seems to have been in a 1963 article in a student newspaper at the Massachusetts Institute of Technology (MIT).

After the first computer systems were linked to multiple users through telephone lines in the early 1960s, *hacker* came to refer to individuals who gained unauthorized access to computer networks, whether from another computer network or, as personal computers became available, from their own computer systems.

Although it is outside the scopes of this book to discuss hacker culture, most hackers have not been criminals in the sense of being vandals or of seeking illicit financial rewards. Instead, most have been young people driven by intellectual curiosity; many of these people have gone on to become computer security architects.

However, as some hackers sought notoriety among their peers, their exploits led to clear-cut crimes. In particular, hackers began breaking into computer systems and then bragging to one another about their exploits, sharing pilfered documents as trophies to prove their boasts.

These exploits grew as hackers not only broke into but sometimes took control of government and corporate computer networks.

One such criminal was Kevin Mitnick, the first hacker to make the "most wanted list" of the U.S. Federal Bureau of Investigation (FBI). He allegedly broke into the North American Aerospace Defense Command (NORAD) computer in 1981, when he was 17 years old, a feat that brought to the fore the gravity of the threat posed by such security breaches.

Concern with hacking contributed first to an overhaul of federal sentencing in the United States, with the 1984 Comprehensive Crime Control Act and then with the Computer Fraud and Abuse Act of 1986.

The scale of hacking crimes is among the most difficult to assess because the victims often prefer not to report the crimes—sometimes out of embarrassment or fear of further security breaches. Officials estimate, however, that hacking costs the world economy billions of dollars annually.

Hacking is not always an outside job—a related criminal endeavour involves individuals within corporations or government bureaucracies deliberately altering database records for either profit or political objectives.

The greatest losses stem from the theft of proprietary information, sometimes followed up by the extortion of money from the original owner for the data's return. In this sense, hacking is old-fashioned industrial espionage by other means.

The largest known case of computer hacking was discovered in late March 2009. It involved government and private computers in at least 103 countries.

The worldwide spy network known as GhostNet was discovered by researchers at the University of Toronto, who had been asked by representatives of the Dalai Lama to investigate the exiled Tibetan leader's computers for possible mal-ware.

In addition to finding out that the Dalai Lama's computers were compromised, the researchers discovered that GhostNet had infiltrated more than a thousand computers around the world.

The highest concentration of compromised systems were within embassies and foreign affairs bureaus of or located in South Asian and Southeast Asian countries.

Reportedly, the computers were infected by users who opened e-mail attachments or clicked on Web page links. Once infected with the GhostNet malware, the computers began "phishing" for files throughout the local network— even turning on cameras and video-recording devices for remote monitoring.

Three control servers that ran the malware were located in Hainan, Guangdong, and Sichuan provinces in China, and a fourth server was located in California.

Computer viruses

The deliberate release of damaging computer viruses is yet another type of cyber-crime. In fact, this was the crime of choice of the first person to be convicted in the United States under the Computer Fraud and Abuse Act of 1986.

On November 2, 1988, a computer science student at Cornell University named Robert Morris released a software "worm" onto the Internet from MIT (as a guest on the campus, he hoped to remain anonymous).

The worm was an experimental self-propagating and replicating computer program that took advantage of flaws in certain e-mail protocols. Due to a mistake in its programming, rather than just sending copies of itself to other computers, this software kept replicating itself on each infected system, filling all the available computer memory.

Before a fix was found, the worm had brought some 6,000 computers (one-tenth of the Internet) to a halt. Although Morris's worm cost time and millions of dollars to fix, the event had few commercial consequences, for the Internet had not yet become a fixture of economic affairs.

That Morris's father was the head of computer security for the U.S. National Security Agency led the press to treat the event more as a high-tech Oedipal drama than as a foreshadowing of things to come. Since then, ever more harmful viruses have been cooked up by anarchists and misfits from locations as diverse as the United States, Bulgaria, Pakistan, and the Philippines.

Denial of service attacks

Compare the Morris worm with the events of the week of February 7, 2000, when "mafia-boy," a 15-year-old Canadian hacker, orchestrated a series of denial of service attacks (DoS) against several e-commerce sites, including Amazon.com and eBay.com.

These attacks used computers at multiple locations to overwhelm the vendors' computers and shut down their World Wide Web (WWW) sites to legitimate commercial traffic.

The attacks crippled Internet commerce, with the FBI estimating that the affected sites suffered $1.7 billion in damages. In 1988 the Internet played a role only in the lives of researchers and academics; by 2000 it had become essential to the workings of the U.S. government and economy. Cyber-crime had moved from being an issue of individual wrongdoing to being a matter of national security.

81

Distributed DoS attacks are a special kind of hacking. A criminal salts an array of computers with computer programs that can be triggered by an external computer user.

These programs are known as Trojan horses since they enter the unknowing users' computers as something benign, such as a photo or document attached to an e-mail. At a pre-designated time, this Trojan horse program begins to send messages to a predetermined site.

If enough computers have been compromised, it is likely that the selected site can be tied up so effectively that little if any legitimate traffic can reach it. One important insight offered by these events has been that much software is insecure, making it easy for even an unskilled hacker to compromise a vast number of machines.

Although software companies regularly offer patches to fix software vulnerabilities, not all users implement the updates, and their computers remain vulnerable to criminals wanting to launch DoS attacks.

In 2003 the Internet service provider PSINet Europe connected an unprotected server to the Internet. Within 24 hours the server had been attacked 467 times, and after three weeks more than 600 attacks had been recorded. Only vigorous security regimes can protect against such an environment.

Despite the claims about the pacific nature of the Internet, it is best to think of it as a modern example of the Wild West of American lore—with the sheriff far away.

Spam

E-mail has spawned one of the most significant forms of cyber-crime—spam, or unsolicited advertisements for products and services, which experts estimate to comprise roughly 50 percent of the e-mail circulating on the Internet.

Spam is a crime against all users of the Internet since it wastes both the storage and network capacities of ISPs, as well as often simply being offensive.

Yet, despite various attempts to legislate it out of existence, it remains unclear how spam can be eliminated without violating the freedom of speech in a liberal democratic polity.

Unlike junk mail, which has a postage cost associated with it, spam is nearly free for perpetrators—it typically costs the same to send 10 messages as it does to send 10 million.

One of the most significant problems in shutting down spammers involves their use of other individuals' personal computers.

Typically, numerous machines connected to the Internet are first infected with a virus or Trojan horse that gives the spammer secret control. Such machines are known as zombie computers, and networks of them, often involving thousands of infected computers, can be activated to flood the Internet with spam or to institute DoS attacks.

While the former may be almost benign, including solicitations to purchase legitimate goods, DoS attacks have been deployed in efforts to blackmail Web sites by threatening to shut them down.

Cyber-experts estimate that the United States accounts for about one-fourth of the 4–8 million zombie computers in the world and is the origin of nearly one-third of all spam.

E-mail also serves as an instrument for both traditional criminals and terrorists. While libertarians laud the use of cryptography to ensure privacy in communications, criminals and terrorists may also use cryptographic means to conceal their plans.

Law-enforcement officials report that some terrorist groups embed instructions and information in images via a process known as steganography, a sophisticated method of hiding information in plain sight.

Even recognizing that something is concealed in this fashion often requires considerable amounts of computing power; actually decoding the information is nearly impossible if one does not have the key to separate the hidden data.

Sabotage

Another type of hacking involves the hijacking of a government or corporation Web site.

Sometimes these crimes have been committed in protest over the incarceration of other hackers; in 1996 the Web site of the U.S. Central Intelligence Agency (CIA) was altered by Swedish hackers to gain international support for their protest of the Swedish government's prosecution of local hackers, and in 1998 the *New York Times*'s Web site was hacked by supporters of the incarcerated hacker Kevin Mitnick.

Still other hackers have used their skills to engage in political protests: in 1998 a group calling itself the Legion of the Underground declared "cyber-war" on China and Iraq in protest of alleged human rights abuses and a program to build weapons of mass destruction, respectively.

Defacing Web sites is a minor matter, though, when compared with the spectre of cyber-terrorists using the Internet to attack the infrastructure of a nation, by rerouting airline traffic, contaminating the water supply, or disabling nuclear plant safeguards.

One consequence of the September 11 attacks on New York City was the destruction of a major telephone and Internet switching centre. Lower Manhattan was effectively cut off from the rest of the world, save for radios and cellular telephones.

Since that day, there has been no other attempt to destroy the infrastructure that produces what has been called that "consensual hallucination," cyberspace. Large-scale cyber-war (or "information warfare") has yet to take place, whether initiated by rogue states or terrorist organizations, although both writers and policy makers have imagined it in all too great detail.

In late March 2007 the Idaho National Laboratory released a video demonstrating what catastrophic damage could result from utility systems being compromised by hackers. Several utilities responded by giving the U.S. government permission to run an audit on their systems.

In March 2009 the results began to leak out with a report in *The Wall Street Journal.* In particular, the report indicated that hackers had installed software in some computers that would have enabled them to disrupt electrical services.

Homeland Security spokeswoman Amy Kudwa affirmed that no disruptions had occurred, though further audits of electric, water, sewage, and other utilities would continue.

85

History of technology

Prehistoric technology

Prehistoric technology is based on the technological developments occurring before written history.

Although a somewhat artificial concept, in that it presupposes that technology advances uniformly world-wide, prehistoric technology generally includes the skills that were practised before the rise of the earliest civilizations in the Middle East and the appearance of cuneiform writing (about the middle of the 4th millennium BC).

This is roughly coincidental with the first known use of copper and bronze, so the working of these metals can be recognized as a prehistoric technology. Iron did not come into use until about 1200 BC; however, many different cultures in Europe used iron long before they had any mastery of written language.

Before the availability of metals, the main building materials were wood and stone. Stone was also used for axes and other tools, flint being skilfully worked to give a cutting edge to knives and arrow heads.

Leather from the hides of slaughtered animals was plentiful, and provided material not only for clothing but also for screens to give protection from the weather and for making buckets and other containers. Basket-work and weaving (see loom) originally used fibres collected in the wild, and date from around 5000 BC.

The most important feature of prehistoric development was the transition from a hunter-gatherer culture to a settled way of life associated with the beginnings of agriculture, in about 9000 BC. The earliest permanent settlement for which much detailed information has come to light is Jericho, in the Jordan Valley, where the original walled city dates from about 8000 BC.

Technology

Technology is the study of the mechanical arts and applied sciences, although the precise meaning of technology has changed over the years and is still to some extent fluid.

Many fundamental technologies--the smelting and working of metals, spinning and weaving of textiles, and the firing of clay, for example--were empirically developed at the dawn of civilization, long before any concept of science existed.

With the advent in about 3000 BC of the first major civilizations in Egypt and Mesopotamia (and a little later in India and China), many new technologies were developed-- irrigation systems, road networks and wheeled vehicles, a pictographic form of writing, and new building techniques.

Other civilizations subsequently became important technological centres, notably those of Greece and Rome, the Arab empire of the 7th to 10th centuries, and the Mayan, Aztec, and Toltec civilizations of meso-America. In the mid-16th century the focus of technological change shifted to Europe, with the beginning of the Scientific Revolution.

This was both an intellectual revolution and a practical one, questioning established dogma, reinterpreting old ideas, and seeking to advance knowledge of the natural world by observation and by experiment.

Initially the new ideas and techniques engendered official persecution, but by the mid-17th century the tide of opinion had changed, as indicated by the formation under royal patronage of the Academie des Sciences in France and the Royal Society in Britain.

By the late 17th century, technology essentially meant engineering, as is indicated by the title of a British book by T. Phillips, published in 1706: *Technology: A Description of Arts, Especially the Mechanical.*

Half a century later, however, Diderot's monumental twenty-eight volume *Encyclopedie* (1751-72) encompassed not only the mechanical but also what he called the liberal arts, including glass-making, agriculture, brewing, and soap-boiling. In the UK in 1866, the teacher and author Charles Tomlinson published his three-volume *Cyclopaedia of Useful Arts, Mechanical and Chemical, Manufactures, Mining, and Engineering*, which, by including the old empirical processes as well as those that had arisen through the application of scientific knowledge, approached the modern concept of technology.

During the 19th century science began to create many new technologies, such as the electric telegraph, the telephone, electricity generation and supply, and photography. The trend continued into the 20th century with the introduction of many goods and services made possible only because of further advances in science.

These have included radio and television, sound recording and reproduction, synthetic fibres, a wide range of pharmaceutical products, nuclear power, and perhaps most important of all, the development of the computer and information technology.

Since the 1970s pollution, depletion of energy resources, and other adverse effects of technology have caused increasing public concern. This has led to the growth of alternative technologies, with an emphasis on renewable energy sources such as solar and wind power, the recycling of raw materials, and the conservation of energy.

Outside the West, only the most basic technology is available to hundreds of millions of people. Tropical agriculture

88

remains resistant to the application of science, and medical technology has made only limited impact in the Third World: according to a recent estimate by the World Health Organization, four-fifths of the world's population still have no regular access to health services of any kind.

For people still locked into subsistence agriculture, the convergence of technology and applied science, which the Western world takes for granted, is largely irrelevant. However, in recent years Western aid has sought to develop appropriate technologies, using local materials and techniques, in partnership with the indigenous peoples.

Telecommunications

Telecommunications refer to the communication of information (usually audio, visual, or computer data) over a distance, transmitted by various means.

Early techniques included signal fires and semaphore; modern systems include telephony, telex, fax radio, television and computer.

Over short distances electrical telegraph or telephone signals can be transmitted via two-wire telephone lines without additional processing.

For longer distances, various techniques of modulation and/or coding at the transmitter, followed by demodulation or decoding at the receiver, are employed to match the transmitted signal to the properties of the telecommunications channel.

Transmission may be to a single receiver or it may be broadcast to many individual receivers; it may be direct or switched through a complex network.

Until recently most telecommunications systems were analogue in nature, but now the message signal commonly undergoes digitization at the transmitter, using pulse code modulation or similar techniques: it is then decoded into usable form (sound, print, video, and so on) at the receiver.

The widespread digitization of telecommunications signals has begun a trend in many countries towards the combination of hitherto separate systems into a single Integrated Services Digital Network (ISDN).

It has also resulted in the convergence of computing and telecommunications. Because of the complexity of modern telecommunications systems, standardization bodies such as the International Telecommunications Union (ITU), and the International Organization for Standardization (ISO) have taken on great importance, particularly in the design of 'open' systems which can be easily interconnected.

Traditionally, telecommunications systems were delivered by a monopoly supplier, usually a branch of government concerned with the postal, telephone, and telegraphic services (in Europe, the PTTs). In the USA the American Telephone and Telegraph was privately owned, but was still subject to government regulations.

As the traditional forms of telecommunications were challenged by computer-based forms of communication, there were calls for the breakup and deregulation of the old telecommunications monopolies.

In 1984 American Telephone and Telegraph, once the largest company in the world, providing four-fifths of the USA's telephones, and nearly all its home and international long-distance services, had its monopoly broken by the government.

It was split into twenty-two local telephone companies grouped into seven regional companies. In Japan the huge Nippon Telegraph and Telephone Company faces similar governmental pressure to break up its monopoly. Markets are also being opened up in Australia and New Zealand, but in most of Europe the retention of a minimum provision of telephone services has been preferred to a policy of greater competition and technological innovation.

The use of sophisticated telecommunications systems is transforming all aspects of business, political, and social life, bringing different societies closer together, and enabling speedy decisions to be taken. (See also communication satellite, electronic mail, optical fibre.)

Electronic mail

Electronic mail (e-mail) is used for sending messages via computer systems.

Many computer systems are now connected to local or wide-area networks and users can communicate with other users anywhere on the network.

Some services offer facilities that allow users to send and receive messages via a microcomputer, a telephone, and a modem.

The sender and receiver need not be on-line at the time; the message is held in a computer mail-box, which the receiver is able to access.

Modem

Modem (*mod*ulator-d*em*odulator) is a computer peripheral used to provide telecommunications links for computer data.

The modem generally converts digital electrical signals into tones which can be transmitted along a telephone line. At the other end of the line, a similar modem operating in reverse converts the frequencies back into digital electrical signals.

Modems work to internationally agreed standards, the most important characteristic being the rate at which the data is transmitted, which is measured in bits per second.

Automation

Automation is the term used for the functioning of automatic machinery and systems, particularly those manufacturing or data-processing systems which require little or no human intervention in their normal operation.

Although the term was first used in 1946 to describe machinery being developed by the Ford Motor Company to move automobile components and work-pieces automatically to and from other machines, the origins of the concept are much older.

During the 19th century a number of machines such as looms and lathes became increasingly self-regulating. At the same time transfer-machines were developed, whereby a series of machine-tools, each doing one operation automatically, became linked in a continuous production line by pneumatic or hydraulic devices transferring components from one operation to the next.

In addition to these technological advances in automation, the theory of 'scientific management', which was based on the early time-and-motion studies of Frederick Winslow Taylor in Philadelphia, USA, in the 1880s was designed by Taylor to enhance the efficiency and productivity of workers and machines.

In the early 20th century, with the development of electrical devices and time-switches, more processes became automatically controlled, and a number of basic industries such as oil-refining, chemicals, and food-processing were increasingly automated.

The development of computers after World War II enabled more sophisticated automation to be used in manufacturing industries, for example in iron and steel production.

The most familiar example of a highly automated system is perhaps an assembly plant for automobiles or other complex products.

Such a plant might involve the automatic machining, welding, transfer, and assembly of parts, using equipment and techniques such as numerically controlled machine-tools, automatically controlled robot arms, and guided vehicles, automated warehousing, materials handling, stock control, and so on.

Advances in automation have been the result of a combination of many factors, including:

- Modifications to the physical layout of production or processing facilities to ease handling;

- Improvements in materials to facilitate manufacturing processes; increasing mechanization of individual processes (the carrying out of tasks by machine rather than human actions), which often necessitates changes to the processes themselves;

- Changes in product design to aid mechanization and mass production; more advanced instrumentation and control systems for both individual machines and for plants as a whole; and

- The adoption of information technology as an integral part of the production process, leading ultimately to the concept of computer-integrated manufacturing.

93

Over the last few decades automation has evolved from the comparatively straightforward mechanization of tasks traditionally carried out by hand, through the introduction of complex automatic control systems, to the widespread automation of information collection and processing.

Whereas in the past automation has involved a high degree of standardization and uniformity in production, the increasing use of information technology has now made it possible to develop more flexible manufacturing systems.

Computer-integrated manufacture

Computer-integrated manufacture (CIM) is the integration of design and production aspects of manufacturing with traditionally separate areas such as planning, purchasing, data processing, financial control, and management support.

CIM has evolved out of earlier techniques such as computer-aided design (CAD), computer-aided manufacture (CAM), numerical control of machine-tools, robotics, flexible manufacturing systems (FMS), and automated materials handling, all of which have been made possible by the use of information technology and computer-based systems.

As a result of the programmability and flexibility of the constituent processes, a CIM system can more easily be directed towards optimizing the effectiveness of the manufacturing operation as a whole, whereas earlier approaches to manufacturing often had to concentrate on maintaining or improving the efficiency of individual aspects only.

Information theory

Information theory (in mathematics) is a theory of communication that concerns the transmission of information by signals.

It covers the capacity of communication channels, the corruption of messages (by 'noise' or interference), and the detection and correction of errors. It is much used in computer and telecommunications systems, but the theory is not specifically electronic.

A simple application is the parity check code for error detection. Suppose each letter of a message is coded as a binary number. For example, the number 1000 might represent A, and 1001 represent B. The A code has an odd number of ones (this is odd parity) and that for B has an even number (even parity).

A fifth digit could be attached to each code to make the parity even. So the code for A would be 10001 and that for B (already even) 10010. A single error in the transmission of these codes (making a one into a zero or vice versa) would alter the parity to odd. The receiver could detect the wrong parity and request retransmission.

With more sophisticated coding the receiver can correct errors, if there are not too many. All error detection and correction uses the concept of redundancy. This is the inclusion of more information in a code than is necessary for the message (for example, the inclusion of the extra digits above).

Human language is highly redundant, as shown by the intelligibility of this corrupt message: mst ppl cn rd ths (most people can read this). Much pioneering work on information theory was done by Claude Shannon in the USA during the 1940s.

95

Practical applications range from the International Standard Book Number (ISBN) on all books, which incorporates a check digit, to the reception of messages from satellites.

Information retrieval

Information retrieval refers to the use of computers to access information stored electronically.

Digital computers were originally developed to perform calculations and process data. Early systems were slow and had limited storage capacity, but with advances in technology, especially the development of fast, high-capacity magnetic disks, computers began to be used to store as well as process data.

For many applications there are significant advantages over traditional paper-based storage. A computer, running suitable retrieval software, can search vast quantities of data and recover information very rapidly.

For example, many databases containing medical, financial, or legal information are available on-line (directly under the control of the central processor) via computer networks or modems over telephone lines.

With the continuing reduction in the cost of storage, and particularly the development of compact discs, information retrieval is likely to become an increasingly important use for computers.

END

Index   *Page*

Bibliography   *ALL BOOKS LISTED BELOW ARE PUBLISHED BY ANDREAS SOFRONIOU*

1. THERAPEUTIC PSYCHOLOGY, ISBN: 978-1-326-34523-5
2. MEDICAL ETHICS THROUGH THE AGES, ISBN: 978-1-4092- 7468-1
3. MEDICAL ETHICS, FROM HIPPOCRATES TO THE 21ST CENTURY ISBN: 978-1-4457-1203-1
4. MISINTERPRETATION OF SIGMUND FREUD, ISBN: 978-1-4467-1659-5
5. JUNG'S PSYCHOTHERAPY: THE PSYCHOLOGICAL & MYTHOLOGICAL METHODS, ISBN: 978-1-4477-4740-6
6. FREUDIAN ANALYSIS & JUNGIAN SYNTHESIS, ISBN: 978-1-4477-5996-6
7. ADLER'S INDIVIDUAL PSYCHOLOGY AND RELATED METHODS, ISBN: 978-1-291-85951-5
8. ADLERIAN INDIVIDUALISM , JUNGIAN SYNTHESIS, FREUDIAN ANALYSIS, ISBN: 978-1-291-85937-9
9. PSYCHOTHERAPY, CONCEPTS OF TREATMENT, ISBN: 978-1-291-50178-0
10. PSYCHOLOGY, CONCEPTS OF BEHAVIOUR, ISBN: 978-1-291-47573-9
11. PHILOSOPHY FOR HUMAN BEHAVIOUR, ISBN: 978-1-291-12707-2
12. SEX, AN EXPLORATION OF SEXUALITY, EROS AND LOVE, ISBN: 978-1-291-56931-5
13. PSYCHOLOGY FROM CONCEPTION TO SENILITY, ISBN: 978-1-4092-7218-2
14. PSYCHOLOGY OF CHILD CULTURE, ISBN: 978-1-4092-7619-7
15. JOYFUL PARENTING, ISBN: 0 9527956 1 2
16. GUIDE TO A JOYFUL PARENTING, ISBN: 0 952 7956 1 2
17. THERAPEUTIC PHILOSOPHY FOR THE INDIVIDUAL AND THE STATE, ISBN: 978-1-4092-7586-2
18. PHILOSOPHIC COUNSELLING FOR PEOPLE AND THEIR GOVERNMENTS, ISBN: 978-1-4092-7400-1
19. CHILD PSYCHOTHERAPY, ISBN: 978-1-326-44169-2
20. HYPNOTHERAPY IN MEDICINE, PSYCHOLOGY, MAGIC, ISBN: 978-1-326-48163-6
21. ART FOR PSYCHOTHERAPY, ISBN: 978-1-326-78959-6
22. SLEEPING AND DREAMING EXPLAINED BY ARTS & SCIENCE, ISBN: ISBN: 978-1-326-81309-3
23. PHILOSOPHY AND POLITICS, ISBN: 978-1-326-33854-1
24. MORAL PHILOSOPHY, FROM SOCRATES TO THE 21ST AEON, ISBN: 978-1-4457-4618-0
25. MORAL PHILOSOPHY, FROM HIPPOCRATES TO THE 21ST AEON, ISBN: 978-1-84753-463-7
26. MORAL PHILOSOPHY, THE ETHICAL APPROACH THROUGH THE AGES, ISBN: 978-1-4092-7703-3
27. MORAL PHILOSOPHY, ISBN: 978-1-4478-5037-3
28. 2011 POLITICS, ORGANISATIONS, PSYCHOANALYSIS, POETRY, ISBN: 978-1-4467-2741-6
29. WISDOM AN ACCUMULATION OF KNOWLEDGE, ISBN: 978-1-326-99692-5
30. MYTHOLOGY LEGENDS FROM AROUND THE GLOBE, ISBN: 978-1-326-98630-8
31. PLATO'S EPISTEMOLOGY, ISBN: 978-1-4716-6584-4
32. ARISTOTLE'S AETIOLOGY, ISBN: 978-1-4716-7861-5
33. MARXISM, SOCIALISM & COMMUNISM, ISBN: 978-1-4716-8236-0
34. MACHIAVELLI'S POLITICS & RELEVANT PHILOSOPHICAL CONCEPTS, ISBN: 978-1-4716-8629-0
35. BRITISH PHILOSOPHERS, 16TH TO 18TH CENTURY, ISBN: 978-1-4717-1072-8
36. ROUSSEAU ON WILL AND MORALITY, ISBN: 978-1-4717-1070-4
37. EPISTEMOLOGY, A SYSTEMATIC OVERVIEW, ISBN: 978-1-326-11380-3
38. HEGEL ON IDEALISM, KNOWLEDGE & REALITY, ISBN: 978-1-4717-0954-8
39. METAPHYSICS FACTS AND FALLACIES, ISBN: 978-1-326-80745-0
40. SOCIAL SCIENCES AND PHILOLOGY, ISBN: 978-1-326-33840-4
41. PHILOLOGY, CONCEPTS OF EUROPEAN LITERATURE, ISBN: 978-1-291-49148-7
42. THREE MILLENNIA OF HELLENIC PHILOLOGY, ISBN: 978-1-291-49799-1
43. CYPRUS, PERMANENT DEPRIVATION OF FREEDOM, ISBN: 978-1-291-50833-8
44. SOCIOLOGY, CONCEPTS OF GROUP BEHAVIOUR, ISBN: 978-1-291-51888-7
45. SOCIAL SCIENCES, CONCEPTS OF BRANCHES AND RELATIONSHIPS ISBN: 978-1-291-52321-8
46. CONCEPTS OF SOCIAL SCIENTISTS AND GREAT THINKERS, ISBN: 978-1-291-53786-4
47. EMPIRES AND COLONIALISM ISBN: 978-1-326-46761-6
48. CYPRUS, COLONISED BY MOST EMPIRES, ISBN, 978-1-326-47164-4
49. PERICLES, GOLDEN AGE OF ATHENS, ISBN: 978-1-326-47592-5
50. TRIANGLE OF EDUCATION TRAINING EXPERIENCE, ISBN: 978-1- 326-82934-6
51. HARMONY IS LOVE FRIENDSHIP SEX, ISBN: 978-1-326-85687-8
52. INTERNATIONAL HUMAN RIGHTS, ISBN: 978-1-326-87348-6
53. ANALYSIS OF LOGIC AND SANITY, ISBN: ISBN: 978-1-326-90604-7
54. INTERNATIONAL LAW, GLOBAL RELATIONS, WORLD POWERS, ISBN: 978-1-326-92921-3
55. MANAGEMENT SCIENCE AND BUSINESS, ISBN: 978-1-326-45508-8
56. ECONOMICS WORLD HOUSE RULES, ISBN: 978-1-326-96162-6
57. POLITICAL SYSTEMS NORMS AND LAWS, ISBN: 978-1-326-97404-6
58. HISTORY OF SYSTEMS, ENGINEERING, TECHNOLOGY, ISBN: 978-1-326-94420-9
59. INFORMATION TECHNOLOGY AND MANAGEMENT, ISBN: 978-1-326-34496-2
60. I.T. RISK MANAGEMENT, ISBN: 978-1-4467-5653-9
61. SYSTEMS ENGINEERING, ISBN: 978-1-4477-7553-9
62. BUSINESS INFORMATION SYSTEMS, CONCEPTS AND EXAMPLES, ISBN: 978-1-4092-7338-7
63. A GUIDE TO INFORMATION TECHNOLOGY, ISBN: 978-1-4092-7608-1
64. CHANGE MANAGEMENT IN I.T., ISBN: 978-1-4092-7712-5
65. FRONT-END DESIGN AND DEVELOPMENT FOR SYSTEMS APPLICATIONS, ISBN: 978-1-4092-7588-6
66. I.T RISK MANAGEMENT, ISBN: 978-1-4092-7488-9
67. I.T. RISK MANAGEMENT – 2011 EDITION, ISBN: 978-1-4467- 5653-9
68. SIMPLIFIED PROCEDURES FOR I.T. PROJECTS DEVELOPMENT, ISBN: 978-1-4092-7562-6

99

69. SIGMA METHODOLOGY FOR RISK MANAGEMENT IN SYSTEMS DEVELOPMENT, ISBN: 978-1-4092-7690-6
70. TRADING ON THE INTERNET IN THE YEAR 2000 AND BEYOND, ISBN: 978-1-4092- 7577
71. STRUCTURED SYSTEMS METHODOLOGY, ISBN: 978-1-4477-6610-0
72. INFORMATION TECHNOLOGY LOGICAL ANALYSIS, ISBN: 978-1-4717-1688-1
73. I.T. RISKS LOGICAL ANALYSIS, ISBN: 978-1-4717-1957-8
74. LOGICAL ANALYSIS OF I.T. CHANGES, ISBN: 978-1-4717-2288-2
75. LOGICAL ANALYSIS OF SYSTEMS, RISKS , CHANGES, ISBN: 978-1-4717-2294-3
76. COMPUTING, A PRÉCIS ON SYSTEMS, SOFTWARE AND HARDWARE, ISBN: 978-1-2910-5102-5
77. MANAGE THAT I.T. PROJECT, ISBN: 978-1-4717-5304-6
78. CHANGE MANAGEMENT, ISBN: 978-1-4457-6114-5
79. MANAGEMENT OF COMMERCIAL COMPUTING, ISBN: 978-1-4092-7550-3
80. PROGRAMME MANAGEMENT WORKSHOP, ISBN: 978-1-4092-7583-1
81. MANAGEMENT OF I.T. CHANGES, RISKS, WORKSHOPS, EPISTEMOLOGY, ISBN: 978-1-84753-147-6
82. THE PHILOSOPHICAL CONCEPTS OF MANAGEMENT THROUGH THE AGES, ISBN: 978-1-4092- 7554-1
83. MANAGEMENT OF PROJECTS, SYSTEMS, INTERNET, AND RISKS, ISBN: 978-1-4092- 7464-3
84. HOW TO CONSTRUCT YOUR RESUMÉ, ISBN: 978-1-4092-7383-7
85. DEFINE THAT SYSTEM, ISBN: 978-1-291-15094-0
86. INFORMATION TECHNOLOGY WORKSHOP, ISBN: 978-1-291-16440-4
87. CHANGE MANAGEMENT IN SYSTEMS, ISBN: 978-1-4457-1099-0
88. SYSTEMS MANAGEMENT, ISBN: 978-1-4710-4907-1
89. TECHNOLOGY, A STUDY OF MECHANICAL ARTS AND APPLIED SCIENCES, ISBN: 978-1-291-58550-6
90. EXPERT SYSTEMS, KNOWLEDGE ENGINEERING FOR HUMAN REPLICATION, ISBN: 978-1-291- 59509-3
91. ARTIFICIAL INTELLIGENCE AND INFORMATION TECHNOLOGY, ISBN: 978-1-291- 60445-0
92. PROJECT MANAGEMENT PROCEDURES FOR SYSTEMS DEVELOPMENT, ISBN: 978-0-952-72531-2
93. SURFING THE INTERNET, THEN, NOW, LATER. ISBN: 978-1--291-77653-9
94. ANALYTICAL DIAGRAMS FOR I.T. SYSTEMS, ISBN: 978-1-326-05786-2
95. INTEGRATION OF INFORMATION TECHNOLOGY, ISBN: 978-1-312-64303-1
96. TRAINING FOR CHANGES IN I.T. ISBN: 978-1-326-14325-1
97. WORKSHOP FOR PROJECTS MANAGEMENT, ISBN: 978-1-326-16162-0
98. SOFRONIOU COLLECTION OF FICTION BOOKS, ISBN: 978-1-326-07629-0
99. THE TOWERING MISFEASANCE, ISBN: 978-1-4241-3652-0
100. DANCES IN THE MOUNTAINS – THE BEAUTY AND BRUTALITY, ISBN: 978-1-4092-7674-6
101. YUSUF'S ODYSSEY, ISBN: 978-1-291-33902-4
102. WILD AND FREE, ISBN: 978-1-4452-0747-6
103. HATCHED FREE, ISBN: 978-1-291-37668-5
104. THROUGH PRICKLY SHRUBS, ISBN: 978-1-4092-7
105. BLOOMIN' SLUMS, ISBN: 978-1-291-37662-3
106. SPEEDBALL, ISBN: 978-1-4092-0521-0
107. SPIRALLING ADVERSARIES, ISBN: 978-1-291-35449-2
108. EXULTATION, ISBN: 978-1-4092-7483-4
109. FREAKY LANDS, ISBN: 978-1-4092-7603-6
110. TREE SPIRIT, ISBN: 978-1-326-29231-7
111. MAN AND HIS MULE, ISBN: 978-1-291-27090-7
112. LITTLE HUT BY THE SEA, ISBN: 978-1-4478-4066-4
113. SAME RIVER TWICE, ISBN: 978-1-4457-1576-6
114. CANE HILL EFFECT, ISBN: 978-1-4452-7636-6
115. WINDS OF CHANGE, ISBN: 978-1-4452-4036-7
116. TOWN CALLED MORPHOU, ISBN: 978-1-4092-7611-1
117. EXPERIENCE MY BEFRIENDED IDEAL, ISBN: 978-1-4092-7463-6
118. CHIRP AND CHAT (POEMS FOR ALL), ISBN: 978-1-291-75055-3
119. POETIC NATTERING, ISBN: 978-1-291-75603-6
120. FREE WILL AND EXTISTENTIALISM, ISBN: 978-0-244-60079-2
121. INSTINCTS AND MECHANISM OF BEHAVIOUR, ISBN: 978-0-244-60468-4
122. PROCESSES OF THINKING. CREATIVITY AND IDEOLOGIES, ISBN: 978- ISBN: 978- 0-244-91126-3
123. PHILOSOPHY AND SCIENCE OF ESCHATOLOGY, ISBN: 978-0-244-63224-3
124. SCIENCE FICTION THE WONDER OF HUMAN IMAGINATION, ISBN: 978-0-244-93409-5
125. HISTORY OF COMPUTER PROGRAMS, ISBN: ISBN: 978-0-244-64246-4
126. Relational Databases and Distributed Systems, ISBN: 978-0-244-07448-7
127. United Nations Organisation Assessment: Global Politics, Relations & Functions, ISBN: 978-0-244-98774-9
128. Psychotherapy and its Plethora of Treatments, ISBN: 978-0-244-39234-5
129. Political Philosophy for Governments & People, ISBN: 978- 0-244-69503-3
130. HELLENISM CLASSICAL & MODERN DIASPORA, ISBN: 978-0-244-10327-9
131. Theology Relationship of Religions & Philosophy, ISBN: 978-0-244-70651-7
132. Mine Own Ideology Idealism Politics, ISBN: 978-0-244-10797-0
133. Academia the Right to Pursue Knowledge, ISBN: 978-0-244-41181-7
134. Interactive Systems, ISBN: **978-0-244-74676-6**